高职高专
国际商务应用
系列教材

国际会展英语（视听说）教程

谢雨彤　舒立志　主　编

黄秀琴　马爱梅　副主编

U0360705

清华大学出版社
北　京

内 容 简 介

本书根据高职高专"工学结合"培养模式编写，根据会展行业的工作环境和岗位要求，营造仿真的工作情境，使学生在逐项完成工作任务的同时，掌握相应的英语词汇、英语表达方法和策划、营销、管理及沟通技巧。全书共八个单元，每个单元包含五至六个模块，通过视频观看、词汇句型练习、角色扮演和口头陈述四个学习步骤，由易到难、循序渐进地让学生掌握国际会展活动中的基本知识和技能，实现会展英语运用能力培养和会展服务能力培养的有机结合。

本书难易程度适中，适合高等职业院校国际商务、会展策划与管理等相关专业教学使用，也可作为会展行业的培训教材，或会展从业人员自学之用。

图书在版编目（CIP）数据

国际会展英语（视听说）教程 / 谢雨彤，舒立志主编. — 北京：清华大学出版社，2021.12（2022.8重印）
高职高专国际商务应用系列教材
ISBN 978-7-302-59342-3

Ⅰ.①国… Ⅱ.①谢… ②舒… Ⅲ.①展览会－英语－听说教学－高等职业教育－教材 Ⅳ.①G245

中国版本图书馆CIP数据核字（2021）第208569号

责任编辑：刘士平
封面设计：傅瑞学
责任校对：赵琳爽
责任印制：朱雨萌

出版发行：清华大学出版社
  网　　　址：http://www.tup.com.cn，http://www.wqbook.com
  地　　　址：北京清华大学学研大厦 A 座　　　邮　　编：100084
  社 总 机：010-83470000　　　　　　　　　邮　　购：010-62786544
  投稿与读者服务：010-62776969，c-service@tup.tsinghua.edu.cn
  质量反馈：010-62772015，zhiliang@tup.tsinghua.edu.cn
  课件下载：http://www.tup.com.cn，010-83470410

印 装 者：三河市龙大印装有限公司
经　　销：全国新华书店
开　　本：185mm×260mm　　　印　　张：11　　　字　　数：237 千字
版　　次：2021 年 12 月第 1 版　　　　　　　印　　次：2022 年 8 月第 3 次印刷
定　　价：46.00 元

产品编号：090416-01

前　言

PREFACE

随着经济全球化的迅速发展,国际会展对于推动国家经济建设发展和促进国民经济效益增长发挥着日益重要的作用,得到了社会各界的高度重视。为适应国际会展行业人才培养需要,本书将理论与实践相结合,构建以工作任务为导向的教学内容体系,融合多学科知识、语言沟通技巧,力求使学生成为满足社会需求的复合型、应用型人才。

本书根据高职高专"工学结合"培养模式编写。编者根据会展行业的工作环境和岗位要求,营造了仿真的工作情境,使学生在逐项完成服务工作任务的同时,掌握相应的英语词汇、英语表达方法和策划、营销、管理及沟通技巧。全书共八个单元,每个单元包含五至六个模块,通过视频观看、词汇句型练习、角色扮演和口头陈述四个学习步骤,由易到难、循序渐进地让学生掌握国际会展活动中的基本知识和技能,实现了会展英语运用能力培养和会展服务能力培养的有机结合。

本书主要有以下特色。

1. 创新性强

本书编者通过走访大量中小型企业,广泛调研中国进出口商品交易会(简称"广交会")、广州国际家具博览会等国际会展活动,确定了会展行业的典型工作过程,并邀请参展商和组展商中经验丰富的行业人士在分析会展工作岗位能力的基础上,共同选取本书内容,实现了岗位任务典型性、真实性及前沿性。本书创新性地设计了对学生实训成果的多元化综合性评价机制,既包括对学生个人会展英语运用和会展服务能力的鉴定,又包括对学生团队项目合作、会展职业道德意识的评价,体现了"课程思政"的宗旨。

2. 趣味性强

本书教学内容丰富生动,典型工作情境以视频动画形式呈现,有助于增强学生学习兴趣,调动学生学习积极性。同时,本书练习形式新颖有趣,包含采访、制作 Vlog、直播等,融知识性、实践性、趣味性于一体,有助于提高学生解决实际问题的能力。

3. 任务性强

本书以会展企业人才岗位需求为依据,以会展商务活动体系中的典型工作任务为导向,从组展商、参展商,以及采购商三个不同角色的真实工作任务出发,编排教学内容,主要内容包括:会展定义及分类、组展商筹办会展、参展商筹备参展、会展接待、展品展示、业务洽谈、展后业务汇报及业务跟进等,学习时间可安排 54 学时左右。本书中,国际会展工作特征体现明显,任务要求明确,学习评价合理。

本书由谢雨彤和舒立志担任主编，黄秀琴和马爱梅担任副主编，赵薇、黄敏、林晓玲、梁极、刘玉贵、余竞超参与编写。具体编写分工如下：广东行政职业学院谢雨彤负责全书的总纂、定稿，并编写第 4 单元；广东轻工职业技术学院舒立志负责编写第1单元；广州软件学院黄秀琴负责编写第 2 单元；江门职业技术学院马爱梅负责编写第3单元；广州城市职业学院赵薇负责编写第 8 单元，并与广东行政职业学院梁极共同编写第 5 单元；仲恺农业工程学院黄敏负责编写第 6 单元；广东培正学院林晓玲负责编写第 7 单元；广东行政职业学院刘玉贵负责收集第 5 单元的资料；广交会广告有限公司总监余竞超负责审核相关专业术语。

编者在对国内外会展行业进行实地调研并对高职学生现有水平和认知规律准确把握的基础上，力求使本书内容与实际工作岗位要求实现无缝对接。本书难易程度适中，适合高职高专商务英语、会展管理、旅游管理、旅游英语等相关专业教学使用，也可作为会展行业的培训教材，或会展从业人员自学之用。

尽管本书编者在特色建设方面做出了许多努力，但由于水平所限，难免有疏漏之处，恳请广大读者批评、指正。本书案例中所有的内容，包括单位名称、人名等均为虚构，如有雷同，纯属巧合。本书在编写过程中得到了广东行政职业学院、广交会广告有限公司、清华大学出版社的大力支持，在此表示衷心感谢。

编　者

2021年7月

Contents 目 录

Unit 1　An Overview of Exhibition

Unit 2　Hosting an Exhibition

Unit 3　Pre-exhibition Preparations

Unit 4　Visitors Reception

Unit 5　Exhibits Presentation

Unit 6　Business Negotiation

Unit 7　Post-show Work

Unit 8　Business Follow-up

An Overview of Exhibition

Learning Objectives

❖ Familiarize with words and expressions on exhibition definition, classification and selection.

❖ Learn to handle the various processes of an exhibition.

❖ Master the specific skills in communication of an exhibition.

❖ Develop the ability to promote trade cooperation.

Warm-up

An exhibition, is a display, show or demonstration of something of beauty, value or particular interest to a target audience. Commercial exhibitions can be categorized into **trade exhibitions**, which bring sellers, buyers, products, goods and services together in particular industrial sectors and **consumer exhibitions**, which are open to the general public and cater to both industries and consumers. When choosing a suitable exhibition, the key is to be clear about your goals. You also need to check its history, consider its visitors and exhibitors, its location and your budget before making the decision. The exhibition, as one of the most effective platforms to establish and maintain client relationships, provides opportunities for companies and individuals to display the latest products. Exhibitions are also commonly used by sellers and buyers to stay updated on their industry trends.

Discuss the following questions in pairs based on the background knowledge above.

1. What do you know about the benefits of attending an exhibition?

2. How many different types of exhibitions do you know?

3. What factors should we take into consideration when choosing an exhibition?

Module 1　Defining an Exhibition

Watch

Task 1　Watch the video and decide whether the following statements are *True* (T) or *False* (F).

1. Ivy Xie is a new salesgirl from SKY Furniture Trading Company.　　　　(　　)

2. Ivy Xie is knowledgeable about exhibitions.　　　　(　　)

3. In general, trade shows are not open to the public.　　　　(　　)

4. The trade show is a different term from the trade fair.　　　　(　　)

5. Canton Fair is held twice a year in Guangzhou.　　　　(　　)

Task 2　Fill in the blanks with the missing words based on the video.

1. Good morning, Ivy. How's _____?

2. I'm fine, thanks. Just trying to _____.

3. Benefits of participating in an exhibition are _____.

4. A trade show, _____, is an event where companies show their products and services.

5. In general, trade shows are B2B type of events. They are not _____.

6. Usually exhibitions cover _____ at a time.

7. Expositions are very large scale events, usually international and covering _____.

8. A fair is a gathering of people for a variety of entertainment or _____.

9. You know, some people, companies or even countries prefer one term to _____.

10. Canton Fair is China's largest trade fair with the highest level, the most complete varieties, and the largest attendance and _____.

Task 3　Watch the video again and choose the best answer to each question.

1. What is Baron Li's job title?

　　A. The sales manager.　　　　　　B. The production manager.

　　C. The marketing manager.　　　　D. The personnel manager.

2. Why are Ivy Xie and Baron Li talking about exhibitions?

A. Because exhibitions are their shared hobbies.

B. Because they are taking an exhibition class in a college.

C. Because they are planning to participate in the China Import and Export Fair.

D. Because they are preparing for a job interview.

3. Which of the following is NOT the benefit of attending an exhibition?

A. It helps you acquire new business.

B. It helps you sell products and services at the booth.

C. It helps you develop new partnerships.

D. It may help you appear in the media.

4. Which one is NOT the feature of expositions?

A. Expositions are open to the public.

B. Expositions are usually international and cover many industries.

C. Expositions may have government support.

D. Expositions cover only one industry at a time.

5. Which statement is true according to the dialogue?

A. Ivy Xie has learned a lot about exhibitions from Baron Li.

B. Baron Li has learned a lot about exhibitions from Ivy Xie.

C. Canton Fair is regularly held every April and October in Guangxi.

D. Canton Fair is the world's largest trade fair.

Task 4   **Work in pairs and summarize the key points of the conversation. Then, try to retell the story in the video.**

Learn

Learn the following *Words & Phrases* and *Sentence Drills*.

Words & Phrases	
adjust *v.* 适应	B2B(Business-to-Business) *abbr.* 企业对企业
exhibition *n.* 展览	B2C(Business-to-Consumer) *abbr.* 企业对消费者
acquire *v.* 获得	differentiate *v.* 区别
exposition(expo) *n.* 博览会	variety *n.* 产品种类
demonstrate *v.* 展示	business turnover 营业额
	keep track of 跟上

China Import and Export Fair 中国进出口商品交易会

trade show/trade fair 交易会

new leads 新客源

Sentence Drills

◆ **Greeting a new employee at the office**

1. Good morning. How's everything going?

   早上好！一切还好吗？

2. I'm Pretty good, thanks.

   我很好，谢谢。

3. Just try to get adjusted. It's hard to keep track of everything around here.

   我正在努力适应呢。在这里事事都要跟上真不容易。

◆ **Talking about exhibitions**

1. What are the benefits of attending an exhibition?

   参展有什么好处？

2. The exhibition is one of the most effective media for establishing and maintaining customer relations.

   展会是建立和维持客户关系最有效的媒介之一。

3. You acquire new business, form new partnerships, and may even appear in the media, which, in turn, generates even more new leads.

   你获得了新的业务，建立了新的合作伙伴关系，甚至可能出现在媒体上，这反过来会带来更多新客源。

4. In general, trade shows are B2B type of events, they are not open to the public.

   一般来说，交易会是 B2B 类型的活动，他们不向公众开放。

5. Usually, an exhibition covers one industry at a time and is aiming at building a general image of the company.

   展会通常一次只涉及一个行业，旨在建立公司的整体形象。

Role-play

Task 1 Alice Wang is a new salesgirl from Guangzhou Rainbow Leather Company who is planning to attend an exhibition. Jack Lee is her supervisor, a sales manager who is knowledgeable about exhibitions. Alice Wang is consulting Jack Lee about exhibitions. Work in pairs and role-play the conversation. Swap roles and practice again. Some sentences are listed for your reference.

1. What are the benefits of attending an exhibition?

2. You acquire new business, form new partnerships, and may even appear in the media, which, in turn, generates even more new leads.

3. Could you tell me the differences between the trade show, exhibition, expo and fair?

4. Trade shows are B2B type of events, they are not open to the public.

5. An exhibition covers one industry at a time and are geared towards building a general image of the company.

6. How can we differentiate trade shows from trade fairs?

Task 2   Suppose you and your partner are salespersons from the same company. You are planning to attend the Canton Fair this October. In pairs, role-play a conversation about attending the Canton Fair. Student A act as a new salesperson, initiate a conversation with Student B, the sales manager.

❖ Student A: try to invent any details to know about exhibitions and Canton Fair from Student B.

❖ Student B: try to answer the questions raised by Student A concerning exhibitions and Canton Fair.

❖ Use as many words and expressions in the Sentence Drills as possible.

Swap roles and practice again. Some sentences are listed for your reference.

1. The Canton Fair is the largest trade fair in China.

2. It has around 24,000 exhibitors showing their latest products over 3 Phases.

3. It is the world's first choice for outsourcing products and components.

4. It attracts more than 200,000 visitors from about 200 countries.

5. Exhibitions help you find products or services to buy.

6. Exhibitions help you find buyers for the products or services that you sell.

7. Exhibitions help you build a professional network with people.

Speak

Read the passage below and discuss the definition and origins of trade shows, then make a presentation about it and figure out how people can benefit from attending trade shows.

Trade Shows: Definition and Origins

There are hundreds of various trade shows taking place every year in the world. Anything can be presented there—from the latest genetic engineering devices and supercars to chicken food and wedding dresses. For every product or service, there is a trade show available, and there is a possibility that YOU—the person who is now reading this article—have participated in at least one of them.

The origin of a trade show goes back to medieval markets, which were usually taking place in a well-known location, such as the main square of the town, and were drawing the attention of both locals and visitors having something to sell or wanting to buy things. Sometimes such a market was the main event of the year in local communities, serving as a meeting point for its members. It was a very convenient way to get the news and exchange information. As time passed by, some of such markets grew bigger. They became more centralized and specialized, finally turned into modern trade shows. And although the way trade shows look today has changed dramatically, the concept remains the same: the trade show is a place to show yourself, acquire new business and exchange news or information on the latest trends.

To put it differently, the trade show is a place to present your business in a way that brings in new clients, strengthens the relationship with existing ones and helps form mutually beneficial partnerships. It is the place where companies can see their position amongst competitors and get ideas on improving their products or services. It is the place where you have a preselected audience for your company message—current and prospective clients, business partners and media, all within easy reach.

（Source：Trade Shows: Definition and Origins. http://www.trade-show-pr.com/2013/02/22/trade-shows-definition-and-origins/, 2021-09-16）

Module 2　Classifying Exhibitions

Watch

Task 1　Watch the video and decide whether the following statements are *True* (T) or *False* (F).

1. Ivy Xie knows nothing about exhibitions. 　　　　　　　　　　　　　　（　　）

2. Sculptures and paintings can be displayed at art exhibitions. 　　　　　（　　）

3. There are three types of commercial exhibitions. 　　　　　　　　　　（　　）

4. Consumer shows are open to the public. 　　　　　　　　　　　　　　（　　）

5. B2C exhibitions are often referred to as trade shows. 　　　　　　　　（　　）

Task 2　Fill in the blanks with the missing words based on the video.

1. I've already had _____ about exhibitions.

2. Well, exhibitions can be broadly _____ three groups.

3. Could you please _____ that?

4. Exhibits may _____ one artist, one group or one theme.

5. Exhibitions _____ historical and scientific themes belong to this category.

6. Business-to-Business exhibitions are often _____ trade shows.

7. They bring together sellers and buyers of products and services in particular _____.

8. Companies gather not only to showcase _____ but also to sell and market them.

9. How about the exhibitions that _____ both industries and consumers?

10. They are open to _____, but admit the public on certain days only.

Task 3 Watch the video again and choose the best answer to each question.

1. Which of the following is true about Ivy Xie?

A. She is an experienced salesgirl.

B. She is knowledgeable about exhibitions.

C. She is consulting Baron Li about exhibitions.

D. She is the sales manager.

2. Which of the following is NOT one of three broad categories of exhibitions?

A. Art exhibitions

B. Interpretive exhibitions

C. Commercial exhibitions

D. Consumer exhibitions

3. Which of the following CANNOT be displayed at art exhibitions?

A. Consumer goods

B. Paintings

C. Sculptures

D. Drawings

4. Which of the following is NOT one of three categories of commercial exhibitions?

A. B2B exhibitions

B. Art exhibitions

C. B2C exhibitions

D. Exhibitions that cater to both industries and consumers

5. Which statement is true according to the dialogue?

A. B2B exhibitions are open to the public.

B. B2C exhibitions are not open to the public.

C. Exhibitions that cater to both industries and consumers are not open to the general public.

D. At consumer shows, companies can sell their products and services.

Task 4 Work in pairs and summarize the key points of the conversation. Then, try to retell the story in the video.

Learn

Learn the following *Words & Phrases* **and** *Sentence Drills.*

Words & Phrases

categorize *v.* 分类

category *n.* 种类，范畴

interpretive *adj.* 阐释性的，解说性的

commercial *adj.* 商业性的

elaborate *v.* 详细阐述

cater *v.* 满足需要

exhibit *v.* 展出

admit *v.* 准许进入

be referred to as 被称为

industrial sectors 工业领域

Sentence Drills

◆ **Talking about exhibition classification**

1. How can we classify exhibitions?

   我们如何对展览进行分类？

2. Exhibitions can be broadly categorized into three groups: art exhibitions, interpretive exhibitions, and commercial exhibitions.

   展览可以大致分为三大类：艺术展览、解说展览和商业展览。

3. Exhibitions related to historical and scientific themes fall into this category.

   与历史和科学主题有关的展览属于这一类。

4. Commercial exhibitions can also be categorized into three major groups: B2B exhibitions, B2C exhibitions, and exhibitions that cater to both industries and consumers.

商业展也可以分为三类：B2B 展、B2C 展，以及同时向行业和消费者开放的展览。

◆ **Talking about commercial exhibitions**

1. B2B exhibitions are often referred to as trade shows, and they bring together sellers and buyers of products and services in particular industrial sectors and are not open to the public.

   B2B 展通常被称为贸易展，它们把特定行业的产品和服务的卖家和买家聚集在一起，而且不向公众开放。

2. B2C exhibitions are often referred to as consumer shows, and they are open to the public.

   B2C 展通常被称为消费展，它们是对公众开放的。

3. At consumer shows, companies gather not only to show their products and services but also to sell and market them.

   在消费类展会上，公司不仅要展示他们的产品和服务，还要进行销售和推广。

4. Such exhibitions exhibit all types of consumer and industrial goods. They are open to the general public, but admit the public on certain days only.

   这样的展览展示了各种类型的消费品和工业产品。它们对公众开放，但只在特定的日子才允许公众进入。

Role-play

Alice Wang is a new salesgirl from Guangzhou Rainbow Leather Company who is planning to attend an exhibition. Jack Lee is her supervisor, a sales manager who is knowledgeable about exhibitions. Alice Wang is consulting Jack Lee about the classification of exhibitions. Work in pairs and role-play the conversation. Swap roles and practice again. Some sentences are listed for your reference.

1. How can we classify exhibitions?
2. Exhibitions can be broadly categorized into three groups: art exhibitions, interpretive exhibitions, and commercial exhibitions.
3. Commercial exhibitions can also be categorized into three major groups: B2B exhibitions, B2C exhibitions, and exhibitions that cater to both industries and consumers.
4. B2B exhibitions are often referred to as trade shows, and they bring sellers and buyers of products and services together in particular industrial sectors and are not open to the public.
5. B2C exhibitions are often referred to as consumer shows, and they are open to the public.
6. A trade show is a great opportunity to raise brand awareness among industry professionals.
7. At consumer shows, companies gather not only to show their products and services but also to sell and market them.
8. Such exhibitions exhibit all types of consumer and industrial goods. They are open to the general public, but admit the public on certain days only.

Speak

Read the passage below and discuss exhibition classification, then make a presentation on how to differentiate among the three types of exhibitions.

Exhibition and Its Classification

Trade shows, exhibitions and expositions are terms popularly used in the exhibition industry. Exhibition, historically a European term, has been adopted by Americans as they become more global, particularly in referring to shows, such as art exhibitions which exhibit in various cities and countries. Expositions are public shows. Trade shows are historically private shows, only open to those involved in the industry. They are "business to business". All these terms describe an activity designed to represent a major industry's marketing event.

In its broadest sense, an exhibition is a display, show or demonstration of something of beauty, value or particular interest to a target audience. Exhibits may be on permanent display or brought together temporarily for a particular event. There are several types of exhibitions.

Business to Business exhibitions

This type of exhibition brings sellers and buyers of products, goods and services together in particular industrial sectors, such as the leather sector, the handicraft sector, the textile sector, the wood sector, etc. However, the degree of specialization varies. They are primarily for business visitors from various levels of trade and industry. They attract a large number of businessmen especially concerned with the show's area of specialization. The exhibitor can be sure that a large number of businessmen will be at the exhibition. For new entries, they can offer the best opportunity to find big buyers, distributors and retailers.

Major multi-type exhibitions

Such exhibitions exhibit all types of consumer and industrial goods. They are open to the general public, but admit the public on certain days only. The audience can be regional, national or international. When exhibiting in this fair, it is difficult to attract worthwhile target visitors, although the audience is huge.

Consumer exhibitions

These are general exhibitions in terms of products shown and audiences' interests. The primary visitors are the public who may come from the immediate area. This type of exhibition is more appropriate for an already established business with distributors and product identity, which are already in retail shops. For example, private exhibitions, in which individual companies or agencies organize their own exhibitions to demonstrate their new goods or services to a selected or invited audience.

Exhibitions provide an opportunity for sellers to explain and demonstrate their products and services directly to potential buyers gathered in one place, and are a cost-effective way of launching new products, penetrating new markets, reinforcing existing customer interest and maintaining or increasing market share. We believe that anyone can enter that expo site and feel a part of something new, and feel a part of the world community.

（Source：李红英. 会展英语实用教程[M].大连：大连理工大学出版社, 2008.）

Module 3　Choosing Exhibitions

Watch

Task 1　**Watch the video and decide whether the following statements are *True* (T) or *False* (F).**

1. Many people make mistakes when choosing exhibitions.　　　　　　　　　（　　）

2. When choosing exhibitions, step one is to be clear about your goals.　　　　（　　）

3. When researching exhibitions, you only need to gather information about them.　（　　）

4. Usually 40%–60% of attendees come from a 200-mile radius of the show location.　（　　）

5. If you are on a tight budget, you should only factor in the registration fees.　　　(　　)

Task 2　Fill in the blanks with the missing words based on the video.

1. I come here again to _____ from you on how to choose the right exhibition to attend.

2. Many choose the biggest and most popular events and hope to get a good _____.

3. You need to define your objectives and _____ what you want to accomplish at trade shows.

4. Do you want to increase leads and _____ relationships with customers?

5. Only after we've clearly defined our objectives should we begin to _____ trade show options.

6. When researching a trade show, you need to gather information on _____ and the local market.

7. Once you've identified a list of potential trade shows, _____ the list by taking a look at their history and past attendance.

8. You need to know how much buying power the trade show has and how well the trade show does _____ sales and networking.

9. Usually 40%–60% of attendees come from a 200-mile _____ of the show location.

10. You should carefully plan your budget and _____ all costs for each exhibition.

Task 3　Watch the video again and choose the best answer to each question.

1. When choosing exhibitions, the first step is to _____.

　　A. clearly define your objectives　　　　　　B. search for trade show options

　　C. check the history of trade shows　　　　　D. consider your budget

2. How can you narrow down a list of potential trade shows according to the dialogue?

　　A. By taking a look at their history and past attendance.

　　B. By knowing how much buying power the trade show has.

　　C. By knowing how well the trade show does in terms of sales and networking.

　　D. All of the above.

3. Usually _____ of attendees come from a 200-mile radius of the show location.

　　A. 30%–50%　　　　　B. 40%–60%　　　　　C. 50%–70%　　　　　D. 60%–80%

4. When making a budget, what costs should you factor in for each exhibition?

　　A. The registration fees, space and exhibition display　　　B. Travel, hotel

　　C. Onsite expenses, giveaways, marketing and promotions　　D. All of the above

5. Which statement is true according to the dialogue?

　　A. If you choose the biggest and most popular exhibition, you can get a good return on investment.

　　B. When researching trade shows, you don't have to estimate how good a fit your product will be for the trade show's audience.

　　C. Location is a very important factor of choosing an exhibition.

　　D. Even if you are on a tight budget, you can still attend the exhibition with success.

Task 4 Work in pairs and summarize the key points of the conversation. Then, try to retell the story in the video.

Learn

Learn the following *Words & Phrases* and *Sentence Drills*.

Words & Phrases

define *v.* 使明确

objective *n.* 目标

option *n.* 选项

identify *v.* 确定

networking *n.* 社交，联络

attendee *n.* 参会人员

radius *n.* 半径范围

figure out 想出，算出

launch a new product 推出新产品

raise awareness 提高知名度

narrow down 缩小

giveaways 赠品

in terms of 从……角度，在……方面

drop off 让……下车

return on investment 投资回报

distribution area 分销区域

target audience 目标观众

factor in 把……考虑在内

onsite expenses 现场费用

Sentence Drills

◆ **Talking about exhibition selection**

1. I come here again to seek advice from you on how to choose the right exhibition to attend.

   我再次来这里是想咨询一下如何选择合适的展会。

2. First of all, you need to clearly define your objectives and figure out what you want to accomplish at the trade show.

   首先，你需要明确你的目标，弄清楚你想在交易会上实现什么。

3. Only after we've clearly defined our objectives should we begin to search for trade show options.

   只有在明确了我们的目标之后，我们才能开始寻找可以选择的展会。

4. When researching trade shows, you need to gather information on the industry and local market, identify your buyers' needs, and estimate how good a fit your product will be for the trade show's audience.

   在搜寻交易会时，你需要收集行业和当地市场的信息，确定买家的需求，并估计你的产品是否适合交易会的观众。

5. Once you've identified a list of potential trade shows, narrow down the list by taking a look at their history and past attendance.

   一旦你确定了潜在的交易会的名单，通过查看他们的历史和过去的参展情况来缩小名单范围。

6. Usually 40%-60% of attendees come from a 200-mile radius of the show location.

   通常40%～60%的参会者都来自以展览地点为中心的200英里范围内。

7. Last but not least is the budget.

   最后但并不意味着不重要的是预算。

Role-play

Alice Wang is a new salesgirl from Guangzhou Rainbow Leather Company who is planning to attend an exhibition. Jack Lee is her supervisor, a sales manager who is knowledgeable about exhibitions. Alice Wang is consulting Jack Lee about how to choose a right exhibition to attend. Work in pairs and role-play the conversation. Swap roles and practice again. Some sentences are listed for your reference.

1. I come here again to seek advice from you on how to choose a right exhibition to attend.
2. First of all, you need to clearly define your objectives and figure out what you want to accomplish at the trade show.
3. Only after we've clearly defined our objectives, we can begin to search for trade show options.
4. Attending a trade show is an investment. And you must make sure that your effort, time, and resources pay off.
5. When researching trade shows, you need to gather information on the industry and local market, identify your buyer needs, and estimate how good a fit your product will be for the trade show's audience.
6. Once you've identified a list of potential trade shows, narrow down the list by taking a look at their history and past attendance.
7. Usually 40%–60% of attendees come from a 200-mile radius of the show location.
8. Last but not least is the budget. You should carefully plan the exhibiting budget and factor in all costs for each exhibition.

Speak

Read the passage below and discuss the crucial factors we should consider when selecting a trade show, then make a presentation on how to choose the right trade show to attend.

How to Choose the Right Trade Show

There are thousands upon thousands of trade shows that take place not only in China but throughout the world. Selecting ones that are right for your niche can be hard, especially when costs are factored into the equation. You have so much time and money that you need spend on trade shows — which is why there can be a lot of pressure behind your final decision.

Here is a quick guide for identifying trade shows that are the right fit for your business.

AUDIENCE

Who is your ideal buyer? Who is your investor? Are they men or women? If you are trying to target a younger crowd, going to a trade show in a big metropolis, like Shenzhen, is basically guaranteed to get you in front of young people. But, if you are targeting an older crowd with more established roots, then bigger and more conventional trade show centers (in places like Guangzhou) might be better suited for you.

INTENT

What is your ultimate goal at a trade show? Do you want to increase leads and sales? Strengthen relationships with customers? Raise awareness for your brand? Depending on your end goal, you might want to consider different sizes of trade shows. If you just want awareness, then massive trade shows can get your name out there. But, if you want a few intimate leads, consider a smaller, more targeted and more exclusive trade show.

HISTORY

You will be taking a chance on a newly established trade show, although, one benefit is that you can probably negotiate a good deal with newer trade shows. For all other more established shows, make sure to check out their history. Here are some topics to research before committing to a trade show: Did the show organizer invest sufficient money and effort into advertising the trade show? How long have they been around? On average, how many people attend their shows? ...This is all the free information you can gather before you decide.

BUDGET

If you are on a tight budget, then not every trade show is going to work for you. Sometimes, you might even have to pick based on the timing of the trade show. There is a discount window when trade shows first announce their dates—you might find yourself simply basing your decision on the trade show dates to ensure you align the discount window with your budget.

Yeah, there can be a lot of trade shows to choose from. Don't feel overwhelmed. Take your time, use the guidelines above, do your research, find the trade shows that are the right fit for your business.

（Source: How to Choose the Right Trade Show. https://blog.exhibitday.com/how-to-choose-the-right-trade-show/, 2021-05-06.）

Module 4　Further Exploration

Role-play

Student A, a journalist for a program from Guangzhou TV—*Share Your Story at the Canton Fair*, is interviewing student B, an experienced exhibitor from SKY Furniture Trading Company about what benefits we can get from attending trade shows and how to get them.

❖ Student A try to invent any details to finish the program.

❖ Student B try to share stories based on the following passage.

❖ Use as many words and expressions in the passage below as possible.

Swap roles and practice again.

Top 5 Benefits of Attending Trade Shows

Trade shows take place in the world in any industry. There is much value in attending a trade show for your industry. Here are the top 5 benefits of attending trade shows.

1. RAISE BRAND AWARENESS

A trade show is a great opportunity to raise brand awareness among industry professionals and key decision-makers. It can be difficult for start-ups to get a foothold in the industry in which they operate. Raising brand awareness at a trade show is a relatively straightforward process. Check out these tips to get it right.

Create eye-catching graphics that engage the audience. Place your brand name, logo, and message strategically throughout the space for maximum impact. Include social media information for potential buyers to find you online. Place your booth close to blue-chip (一流的) companies. This will enhance your brand as it gives attendees the impression that you are one of the industry leaders. It also has the benefit of a steady flow of foot traffic.

2. FORGE BUSINESS RELATIONSHIPS

Everybody needs help no matter how big or great they are as a company. Forging alliances with other industry-related companies can help you enter vertical markets that you would not break into otherwise. Here are some ideas on how to increase your networking opportunities.

Take a look at the exhibition schedule for social events, such as parties, lunch breaks, and other gatherings. These are great side events that allow you to mingle with industry leaders in a relaxed setting and potentially exchange contact information.

3. HIGHLY TARGETED LEADS

Your sales team will love the trade show environment because a large crowd of highly targeted buyers is herded under one roof. Attendees who make the effort to attend a trade show do so because they are actively looking to buy the right products for their needs. The sales team simply needs to highlight the positive aspects of your products effectively to close a sale. Refer to these tips on how to sell at a trade show.

Set up your trade show booth around your flagship products and highlight the benefits to the consumer. Try to close the deal on the spot. For deals that you cannot close on the spot, set up an appointment after the event for another chance to persuade the lead.

4. COMPETITOR ANALYSIS

A trade show exposes the strategies and best offerings of all the top brands in the industry. Take a walk around the show floor and see what other companies are doing to attract customers. Here are some suggestions for executing effective competitor analysis.

As much as your industry and competitors will tolerate, do in-depth research in their booths. Learn as much as possible about what they have deemed to be their most significant offerings. Keep notes on everything you learn in an organized manner and focus on the booths that are attracting the most attention.

5. EDUCATION

Trade shows are usually filled with a lot of educational sessions that help you explore and learn about the industry you operate in. Keeping up-to-date with the latest developments and new technologies enables you to plot a course for your business to be competitive.

Look at the schedule to find out what sessions are taking place during the event. Prioritize sessions that are most related to your business and determine how you can fit them into your schedule.

Take notes during the educational events to remember actionable information to be applied once you get back to the office. Network with industry leaders at competing booths. Develop a relationship and they might share some insight that might help you improve your products.

Now that you have learned about the benefits of attending trade shows—providing new business, increasing brand awareness, presenting networking opportunities, and giving the chance to learn more about the industry you conduct business in. Pick out a trade show that matches your product range and begin planning for success!

（Source:Top 5 Benefits of Attending Trade Shows. https://evoexhibits.com/top-5-benefits-of-attending-trade-shows/,2021-07-06.）

Module 5 Simulation Workshop

Step 1 Project Background

Ivy Xie, the salesgirl, and Baron Li, the sales manager are both from SKY Furniture Trading Company, visited Guangzhou International Convention and Exhibition Center which is home to China's most important trade fair, the Canton Fair along with numerous other major international and domestic trade events. They are planning to attend a furniture exhibition there. The marketing manager John Wang and the receptionist Nina Zhang from Exhibition Center are responsible for receiving Ivy and Baron and introducing different types of exhibitions held at the Exhibition Center. They are talking about how to choose a suitable exhibition for them to attend.

Step 2   Suggested Preparations

1. Role Assignment

Build a team with 4 students. Then, decide roles for each team member who undertakes the corresponding task, such as:

introducing Exhibition Center and different types of exhibitions held at the Center;

introducing how to choose a suitable exhibition for exhibitors to attend;

introducing SKY Furniture Trading Company, including business scope, history, achievements, certificates, exhibition objectives, etc.

2. Collect Information

Collect necessary information and get ready for the presentation.

3. Rehearse and Make Improvements

Have a rehearsal about the presentation and make improvements if necessary.

Step 3   Video Shooting

Shoot a video about the sum-up meeting. Hand in your video and your teacher will rank and award the top 3 videos.

❖ **Self-assessment**

Assess according to the following table and find out what progress you have made.

Learning Assessment

Assessment Content	Assessment Standard	Total Score	Self-Assessment Result	Your Score
Listening Activity	I can get the right answer for the listening tasks.	10		
	I can grasp the general idea of the listening materials.	10		
	I can detect the details of the listening materials.	5		
	I can take notes when listening to classmates' presentations.	5		

Continued

Assessment Content	Assessment Standard	Total Score	Self-Assessment Result	Your Score
Role-play and Speaking Activity	I can use the skills and conduct the tasks required in this unit.	5		
	I can talk about the subject and its relevant information in this unit.	5		
	I can play well in the role-play.	10		
	I can express and present my ideas about the subject and its relevant information.	10		
Reading Activity	I can understand the main idea of the text.	5		
	I can use the words, phrases and sentence patterns in the text to finish the speaking exercises.	5		
Pronunciation	I can pronounce the new words correctly with a standard tone and rhythm.	10		
Fluency and Coherence	I can use a range of connectives and discourse markers to express my ideas with logic and coherence.	10		
Grammatical Range and Accuracy	I can use a mix of simple and complex grammatical structures, but with limited flexibility.	10		
Total		100		

Hosting an Exhibition

Learning Objectives

❖ Familiarize with words and expressions on planning, publicizing an exhibition, and inviting exhibitors.

❖ Learn to talk about publicizing skills and inviting exhibitors in English.

❖ Master the listening skills concerning publicizing exhibitions and inviting exhibitors.

❖ Develop basic etiquette in inviting exhibitors.

Warm-up

No matter which industry you are working in, you may have experience of attending exhibitions. An exhibition is an event that collectively displays different arts, products or skills. Both individuals and businesses take part in this event to reach specific goals. There are various types of exhibitions specially organized to cater to the needs of the participants. Exhibitions can be categorized into museums, art exhibitions, trade exhibitions and consumer exhibitions. They can be commercial or non-commercial. Trade shows are events between organizations and businesses. They are designed to let the participants showcase their products and services and see if they can gain the interest of another company. They are commercial exhibitions but only those invited can attend. Consumer exhibitions take full advantage of different companies to expose their products and services to the public. The idea behind this event is to attract the public to buy their products or services.

Discuss the following questions in pairs based on the background knowledge above.

1. What is an exhibition?

2. Can art exhibitions be commercial?

3. What is different between trade shows and consumer exhibitions?

Module 1　Planning an Exhibition

Watch

Task 1　Watch the video and decide whether the following statements are *True* (T) or *False* (F).

1. Kathy and Alice will be involved in a big project. ( )

2. Kathy doesn't have any experience in organizing exhibitions. ( )

3. This is the first time for Kathy to organize such a big trade Fair. ( )

4. They need to set up a good team because the scale of the Canton Fair is huge. ( )

5. Kathy will give the exhibition proposal to David by the end of next week. ( )

Task 2　Fill in the blanks with the missing words based on the video.

1. I'd like you and Rachel to be _____ in a big project.

2. We need to _____ an exhibition proposal so as to get the ball rolling as quickly as possible.

3. Could you please give me some _____?

4. You have already gained a lot of _____ in organizing exhibitions.

5. We need to set up a good team with those people who can work _____ and also think independently.

6. Try to simplify the steps and make some _____.

7. As you know, making exhibitors more _____ is one of our service goals.

8. I have already _____ this down.

9. The last but not the least thing is the _____.

10. If things are _____ early in the planning process, we can avoid any last-minute problems.

Task 3　Watch the video again and choose the best answer to each question.

1. _____ is the first thing that Kathy should do.

A. Writing "Exhibition Introduction"

B. Writing "The Application Procedure"

C. Building a team

D. Making budget

2. Which is NOT the important thing mentioned in the dialogue when organizing Canton Fair?

   A. The time of the opening ceremony   B. Providing conveniences for exhibitors

   C. Building a good team   D. Making the budget

3. Which statement is true according to the dialogue?

   A. They do a lot of modifications in writing the "Exhibition Introduction" part.

   B. They will try to make exhibitors more convenient.

   C. The exhibition fees for domestic exhibitors and overseas exhibitors are the same.

   D. The budget is only used for publicity expenses.

Task 4 **Work in pairs and summarize the key points of the conversation. Then, try to retell the story in the video.**

Learn

Learn the following *Words & Phrases* and *Sentence Drills*.

Words & Phrases	Sentence Drills
involve *v.* 参与，涉及	◆ **Talking about organizing exhibitions**
proposal *n.* 计划书，方案	1. I think building a team of about 10 members with the necessary skills and experience is the first thing you should do.
assemble *v.* 召集	
scale *n.* 规模	
modification *n.* 修改	我认为首先要做的事是组建一支有必要能力和经验的10人左右的队伍。
application *n.* 申请	
improvement *n.* 改进	2. Since the scale of the Canton Fair is huge, we need to set up a good team with those people who can work responsibly and also think independently.
convenience *n.* 便利	
domestic *adj.* 国内的	
budget *n.* 预算	
thoughtful *adj.* 考虑周全的	由于广交会的规模很大，我们需要建立一支好的队伍，队伍的成员必须有责任心和能独立思考。
publicity *n.* 宣传	
personnel *adj.* 人力的	
work out 制订	3. As for the detailed application procedure, try to simplify the steps and make some improvements.
get the ball rolling 让一切动起来，开始（工作）	
write down 写下来，记下来	至于申请参展详细步骤，请尽量简化步骤并改善申请流程。
in charge of 负责	
	4. We should make every penny count.
	我们要把每一分钱都花在刀刃上。

Role-play

Student A, the manager of SGS, a famous international convention and exhibition company. He is making a plan for the China International Furniture Fair. And he is discussing the exhibition proposal with Student B, his colleague. Swap roles and practice again. Some sentences are listed for your reference.

1. We need to work out an exhibition proposal to get the ball rolling as quickly as possible.

2. I think building a team of about 10 members with the necessary skills and experience is the first thing you should do.

3. As you know, making the process more convenient is one of our service goals.

4. The last but not the least thing is the budget.

5. You have to learn to allocate the right budget to gather enough resources needed to create a successful exhibition.

6. If things are arranged early in the planning process, we can avoid last-minute problems.

Speak

Read the following news report and search for more information from the Internet. Try to make a presentation on the online exhibition. Your presentation should follow the three parts below.

1. What is online exhibitions' purpose?

2. What are the benefits of the online exhibition?

3. What is the future of online exhibitions?

The Online Session of the Canton Fair

According to the Ministry of Commerce, the 127th session of the China Import and Export Fair (the Canton Fair) was held online for the first time in its 62-year history, which lasted for ten days, from June 15 to 24, 2020.

Due to the global travel restrictions caused by the COVID-19 pandemic, the online session of the Fair is a way to cushion and ensure the stability of foreign trade and investment, showing the role of the fair in an all-round opening-up platform.

The Ministry of Commerce emphasized the equal importance of import and export, promoting the matching of production, supply and sales. The online Fair provided services including online exhibitions, promotion, business docking and negotiations. During the online Canton Fair, people could visit the online showrooms to find out the products. For many enterprises, they even introduce their latest products by live broadcast. What is more, people can visit the website of the online Fair to find out information about the factory capacity, working conditions and instructions, production equipment at the factory, warehouse and so on. According to the news reports, this online session of the Fair had attracted around 26,000 enterprises in 16 categories with 1.8 million products.

With the higher online technology, enterprises and merchants have offered better services for customers from all over the world, making the online session a success. Thus, the world will witness the prospect of the online exhibition with advanced technology, seeing new ways to hold the "new" Canton Fair.

Module 2   Publicizing an Exhibition

Watch

Task 1   Watch the video and decide whether the following statements are *True* (T) or *False* (F).

1. Rachel has a lot of experience in publicizing exhibitions.   (   )
2. We should call exhibitors before sending them invitations.   (   )
3. Regular exhibitors are as important as new exhibitors.   (   )
4. They never run ads on TV.   (   )
5. They will ask for help from the Ministry of Commerce of P. R. C. and the People's Government of Guangdong Province to share the link of publicizing videos.   (   )

Task 2   Fill in the blanks with the missing words based on the video.

1. Please take your _____ and come to my office.
2. I'm ready to _____ everything you give to me.
3. It is time to _____ it now.
4. I have little _____ in publicizing exhibitions.
5. We need to _____ our regular exhibitors and send them the invitations via E-mail.
6. We will call them to _____ whether they have received our invitation.
7. I think it is _____ to call them at least three days after sending the invitations.
8. There are always some new companies need our _____ to promote their products.
9. But how can we develop new exhibitors _____ ?
10. What's more, it is very _____.

Task 3   Watch the video again and choose the best answer to each question.

1. When is the proper time to call regular exhibitors after sending them the invitations?

   A. at least three days   B. at least two days

   C. at least a week   D. Not mentioned

2. If the new exhibitors have no idea to design the display, we can _____.

    A. ignore them   B. design for them

    C. recommend some reliable exhibition designing companies to them   D. Not mentioned

3. Which statement is true according to the dialogue?

    A. Running ads in the newspaper, on TV as well as the Internet is not expensive.

    B. They will show some publicizing videos on some online platforms.

    C. There are always some new companies that need our assistance to promote their products.

    D. There will be only one team to be responsible for contacting exhibitors.

Task 4 **Work in pairs and summarize the key points of the conversation. Then, try to retell the story in the video.**

Learn

Learn the following *Words & Phrases* and *Sentence Drills*.

Words & Phrases

organization *n.* 组织，机构

distribute *v.* 分派，分发

assignment *n.* 任务

publicize *v.* 宣传

guidance *n.* 指导

assistance *n.* 帮助

promote *v.* 推广

effective *adj.* 有效的

inexperienced *adj.* 经验不足的

recommend *v.* 推荐

reliable *adj.* 可靠的

take up 开始从事；占据（时间，地方）

make sure 确保

Sentence Drills

◆ **Talking about ways of publicizing**

  1. Running ads in the newspaper, on TV as well as Internet, and some other mainstream media is very costly.

    在报纸、电视、网络以及其他主流媒体上投放广告是非常昂贵的。

  2. How about showing some publicizing videos on some online platforms?

    不如在一些网络平台上播放宣传视频吧？

  3. We can also ask assistance from local governments to share the link of publicizing videos.

    我们可以向当地政府寻求帮助，让他们分享宣传视频的链接。

◆ **Expressing the experience of doing sth.**

  1. We have no/little/ a lot experience in promoting products.

    我们没有 / 有很少 / 有很多推广产品的经验。

  3. She is very experienced.

    她很有经验。

  3. Sam is inexperienced.

    山姆经验不足。

Role-play

Student A is introducing the online trade fair to his regular exhibitor Student B. Swap roles and practice again. Some sentences are listed for your reference.

1. Since there is a Covid-19 epidemic, I am calling to give you detailed information about the online Canton Fair.

2. If you want to promote your products and establish new business relationships, the Canton Fair provides a great opportunity to gain much exposure to a high volume of potential clients, no whether it is a traditional trade fair or an online one.

3. The online exhibition not only increases the confidence of overseas buyers in the supply chain stability but also provides supports for the global resumption of work and production.

Speak

Read the table below and make a presentation on how to promote an exhibition effectively.

Ways to Promote	Features
Email and Invitation Letter	● It will help in bringing new potential exhibitors, especially those who are still hesitant about whether they should attend. ● Strong, thoughtful relationship-building strategies can be effective for a successful trade show.
Direct Mail	● It will provide the exhibitors with complete information about the services and the requirements. ● It is a great medium for capturing attention and extending a personal touch with existing customers. It will help the customer get the right information about the current trade show.
Advertising	● It is directly linked to marketing. Good advertising can create interest and also tell more and more individuals about the exhibition to be launched. ● Advertising is not limited to magazines, newsletters and brochures, but rather extended to virtually any item that will accept print.
Telemarketing	● This has become a bit more dangerous with the No-Not-Call list. ● If you have any contact with someone in the last six months, there should be no problem with you making that phone call.

Module 3   Inviting Exhibitors

Watch

Task 1   Watch the video and decide whether the following statements are *True* (T) or *False* (F).

1. The Canton Fair is held three times a year. (   )

2. George has decided to attend the 128th Canton Fair before getting Rachel's call. (   )

3. Rachel will send George the registration form and George has to send back the forms before the registration deadline. (   )

4. The spring Session normally lasts from April 15th to May 5th and the autumn session from October 15th to November 5th. (   )

5. During the 126th session, there were 26,808 standard booths. (   )

Task 2   Fill in the blanks with the missing words based on the video.

1. Well, the China Import and Export Fair, also known as the Canton Fair, is _____ in the Spring of 1957.

2. The Canton Fair is a _____ international trading event with the longest history, the largest scale, the most complete exhibit variety, the largest buyer attendance in China.

3. Various types of business activities such as economic and technical cooperation and exchanges, commodity inspection, insurance, transportation, advertising, _____ , etc. are also carried out in flexible ways.

4. More and more business people from all over the world are gathering in Guangzhou, _____ business information and developing business relations.

5. The Canton Fair is held two _____ a year, three phases each session.

6. Maybe this year I can _____ the Autumn session.

7. During 126th session there were 60,676 booths and the exhibition area of one session _____ 1,185,000 square meters.

8. May I know how many _____ and visitors attended it?

9. The export volume _____ CNY 207.09 billion (USD 29 billion).

10. Actually there were a great number of _____ and orders made after the fair.

Task 3   Watch the video again and choose the best answer to each question.

1. When was Canton Fair inaugurated?

   A. In the Autumn of 1959   B. In the Spring of 1959

   C. In the Spring of 1957   D. In the Autumn of 1957

2. How many booths were there at the 126th Canton Fair?

   A. 60,767   B. 16,767   C. 16,676   D. 60,676

3. How long does it last for each phase?

   A. 6 days   B. 7 days   C. 5 days   D. 8 days

4. How many exhibitors and visitors were there at the 126th Canton Fair?

   A. 35,642 and 210,000   B. 25,642 and 200,000

   C. 25,632 and 300,000   D. 35,632 and 300,000

5. What's the export volume of the 126th Canton Fair?

   A. USD 29.218 billion   B. USD 29 billion

   C. USD 39.218 billion   D. USD 39.288 billion

Task 4   Work in pairs and summarize the key points of the conversation. Then, try to retell the story in the video.

Learn

Learn the following *Words & Phrases* and *Sentence Drills*.

Words & Phrases

committee *n.* 委员会

commodity *n.* 商品，日用品

inaugurate *v.* 开始，开创

enterprise *n.* 公司，企业

credibility *n.* 可信，可靠

financial *adj.* 金融的，财务的

capability *n.* 才能，性能

institution *n.* 机构，学院

inspection *n.* 检查，视察

insurance *n.* 保险

transportation *n.* 交通，运输

consultation *n.* 咨询，请教

transaction *n.* 交易，事务

download *v.* 下载

registration *n.* 注册，登记

take part in 参加

the application form 申请表

the official website 官方网站

Sentence Drills

◆ **Answering phone calls from the Organizing Committee of Chinese Export Commodities Fair**

1. Can I speak to George Parker?

   我可以请乔治·帕克接电话吗？

2. I have received your invitation letter and I am planning to attend the 128th Canton Fair, but I'd like to know something more about it.

   我已经收到你们的邀请函，计划参加第128届广交会，但我还想进一步了解广交会的相关信息。

3. More and more business people from all over the world are gathering in Guangzhou, exchanging business information and developing business relations.

越来越多的来自世界各地的商务人士聚集在广州，交流商务，增进友谊。

4. The Canton Fair is held two sessions a year, three phases each session.

广交会一年举行两次，每次有三期。

Role-play

Role-play a conversation about visiting an exhibition hall (Pazhou Complex琶洲展馆) in Guangzhou. Student A is required to fill in the form according to the information shared by student B.

Question	Answer
Name of the Exhibition Hall	
Location(地理位置)	
Appearance and Design(外观和设计)	
Transportation (交通)	
History	
Facilities	
Exhibitions and Events	

Swap roles and practice again. Some sentences are listed for your reference.

1. The Pazhou Complex covers a total area of about 700,000 square meters with 16 exhibition halls, ranking it as the largest exhibition center in Asia.

2. The unparalleled wave-like rooftop resembles the flowing of Pearl River and also displays the dynamic spirit of Guangzhou.

3. You can arrive at the Canton Fair Complex directly by taking Metro Line 8 and get off at the Xingangdong Station or the Pazhou Station.

Speak

Read the passage below and make a presentation on why exhibitors exhibit and why visitors visit the Guangzhou International Furniture Fair. Some sentences are listed for your reference.

1. CIFF covers the entire industry chain including home furniture, home decor & home textile, outdoor & leisure, office furniture, commercial furniture, hotel furniture and furniture machinery

& raw materials.

2. It will help companies explore both domestic and overseas markets, contributing to the development of China and the world's home furnishing industry.

3. CIFF covers the entire industry chain at home and abroad, gathering 4334 domestic and overseas furniture brands.

4. CIFF aims to help exhibitors and visitors grasp the latest trends of the home furniture industry, offering a feast of fashion and trends for the entire industry.

Why Exhibit?

Preferred Choice for Product Launch and Trade

Founded in 1998, the China International Furniture Fair (Guangzhou/Shanghai) (short for "CIFF") has been successfully held for 45 sessions. Starting from September 2015, it takes place annually in Pazhou, Guangzhou in March, and Hongqiao, Shanghai in September, radiating into the Pearl River Delta and the Yangtze River Delta, the two most dynamic commercial centers in China. CIFF covers the entire industry chain including home furniture, home decor & home textile, outdoor & leisure, office furniture, commercial furniture, hotel furniture and furniture machinery & raw materials. The spring and autumn sessions host over 6000 brands from China and abroad, gathering over 340,000 professional visitors in total. CIFF creates the world's most preferred one-stop trading platform for product launch, domestic sales and export trade in the home furnishing industry.

Worldwide Attendance

CIFF(Guangzhou) targets audiences from different industries and sectors by sending tailored invitations through different channels. It attracts more than 190,000 importers/exporters, dealers, retailers, brand chain stores, designers, architects, real estate developers, and other professional visitors from over 200 countries and regions annually.

Global Promotion

CIFF conducts promotion activities in famous furniture exhibitions in the world including the High Point Market, Milan Furniture Fair and Imm Cologne as well as in emerging furniture markets such as the Middle East, Latin America, Japan, Korea and Southeast Asia. CIFF advertises in Chinese key furniture distribution hubs and local furniture malls. It is covered by over 1,100 domestic and overseas mainstream channels and media including Google, Facebook, Baidu, Sina, Netease, Tencent, Sohu, Furniture Today, Mobelmarkt and Commercial Interior Design.

Sets the Trend

Over the past twenty-three years, CIFF has adhered to the mandate of "prioritizing exhibitors and visitors". As an integrated functional platform of channel maintenance, trend release, industry exchange and trade facilitation, CIFF brings more and more value to the industry and enterprises. In the future, CIFF will always be dedicated to creating a brand new lifestyle and setting the industry trend. CIFF will further promote the consumption market upgrade and infuse more vitality to the industry. It will help companies explore both domestic and overseas markets, contributing to the development of China and the world's home furnishing industry.

（Source: http://ciff-gz.com.com /en/visitors/why-visit, 2021-05-06.）

Why Visit?

Comprehensive Products

CIFF covers the entire industry chain including home furniture, home decor & home textiles, outdoor & leisure, office furniture, commercial furniture, hotel furniture and furniture machinery & raw materials.

Diversified Brands

CIFF(Guangzhou) gathers 4334 domestic and overseas furniture brands. Leading enterprises bring shining new products while newly emerging brands showcase the charm of vitality. Top brands of China and broad present the best under the same roof, together creating the best commercial platform for product launch, domestic sales and export trade.

Exciting Activities

CIFF holds a series of exciting design activities, forums and launch events to help exhibitors and visitors grasp the latest trends of the home furniture industry, offering a feast of fashion and trends for the entire industry.

Friendly Services

CIFF keeps improving the on-site service. With convenient entry, humanized visiting route, hall facilities, VIP reception, catering, hotel and transportation services, CIFF offers a friendly experience to all participants.

Module 4　Further Exploration

Role-play

Student A, a journalist for a program from Guangzhou TV—*Green Exhibition*, is interviewing student B, a staff from the China International Furniture Fair (Guangzhou) about the "Green Exhibition" held by China International Furniture Fair (Guangzhou)-Phase 2.

❖ Student A is trying to invent any details to finish the program.

❖ Student B is trying to share details based on the following passage.

❖ Use as many words and expressions in the following passage as possible.
Swap roles and practice again.

 China International Furniture Fair (Guangzhou) –Phase 2 (July 27-30,2020)

The Initiative on "Green Exhibition":
Create a Green Exhibition, Implement Green Development

All Exhibitors and Builders:

To thoroughly implement the spirit of the 18th and 19th CPC National Congress, further promote comprehensive resource conservation and recycling, reduce the energy and material consumption, improve the utilization and regeneration of resources and create a green CIFF, the 45th CIFF strongly advocates the concept of "Green Exhibition". All exhibitors and builders shall strengthen the construction of green CIFF from the aspects of green move-in, green participation and green moveout and finally achieve the goal of "Green Exhibition".

I　Green Move-in

Exhibitors shall use non-toxic, harmless, recyclable and eco-friendly materials. The main frames shall be of profiles (steel structures, aluminum profiles). No special board waste shall be generated. No paint or lime wash shall be used. The eco-friendly and energy-efficient lamps shall be used for booth lighting.

II　Green Participation

1. Exhibitors are encouraged to use green exhibition appliances and equipment that meet national environmental standards to achieve green participation.

2. Exhibitors are encouraged to use recyclable or degradable packaging materials to reduce the impact on the environment.

3. Exhibition personnel are encouraged to attend the exhibition by taking public transport as much as possible to achieve green commuting.

4. Control the light and noise pollution during the exhibition to create a comfortable environment for negotiation.

5. Implement waste sorting and recycling to reduce the amount of waste.

III　Green Move-out

1. Comply with the state safety production laws and regulations, strictly enforce the operating procedures and operate according to rules and regulations; ensure construction safety, protect the personal safety of construction personnel and prohibit the rash and rough construction.

2. Priority shall be given to the recycling and utilization of the degradable, recyclable and

disposable materials to reduce the generation of waste boards and garbage.

The 45th China (Guangzhou) International Furniture Fair

December 2019

（Source:https://api.ciff-gz.nanyouquan.net/uploads/files/ba4833d04c2bddf67722f22a8a663b23.pdf, 2021-05-06.）

Module 5   Simulation Workshop

Step 1   Project Background

Work in pairs and make an invitation letter for the 128th Canton Fair. You need to emphasize the services and the uniqueness of the fair to attract the exhibitors. Note that the invitation letter should be concise and laid out in short, business-like paragraphs, and it should be sent at least one week before the opening of the exhibition. Related information about the 128th Canton Fair is as follows.

Phase 1: October 15-19, 2020

Electronics & Household Electrical Appliances; Lighting Equipment; Vehicles & Spare Parts Machinery; Hardware & Tools; Building Materials; Chemical Products; Energy

Phase 2: October 23-27, 2020

Consumer Goods; Gifts; Home Decorations

Phase 3: October 31-November 4, 2020

Textiles & Garments; Shoes; Office Supplies, Cases & Bags, Recreation Products; Food; Medicines, Medical Devices, Health Products

Venue: China Import and Export Fair Complex

Add: No.382 Yuejiang Zhong Road, Guangzhou ,510335, China

Reminder for Overseas Exhibitors

The Exhibitor Entry badge is the only official admission to the Canton Fair. If you don't have it, please apply for it via the Easy Exhibitor system on the Canton Fair's official website and get it in /at the International Pavilion Exhibitors Badge Service Center.

Required documents for Getting Exhibitor Entry Badge

1. Valid Original Personal Documents (Overseas Passport, H. K./ Macao Home-return Permit, Taiwan Compatriot Travel Certificate, Valid ID as Overseas Chinese or a Chinese Passport with overseas employment visa valid for over one year).

2. A recent passport photo in the size of 5cm × 4cm

3. Business Card

As for more details about the Exhibitors Badges Application, please visit the Easy Exhibitor system on the Canton Fair Official Website for more details.

Website: www.cantonfair.org.cn, www.cftc.org.cn

Tel: 40000-888-999 (On Chinese Mainland), 86-20-28888999 (Outside the Chinese Mainland)

Email: internationalpavillion@cantonfair.org.cn

Step 2   Suggested Preparations

1. Roles Assignment

Build a team with 5 students. Then, decide roles for each team member who undertakes the corresponding task, such as introducing the Canton Fair (including history, function, achievements, etc.).

2. Collect Information

Collect necessary information and get ready for presentation.

3. Rehearse and Make Improvements

Have a rehearsal about the presentation and make improvements if necessary.

Step 3   Video Shooting

Shoot a video about the sum-up meeting. Hand in your video and your teacher will rank and award the top 3 videos.

❖ **Self-assessment**

Assess according to the following table and find out what progress you have made.

Learning Assessment

Assessment Content	Assessment Standard	Total Score	Self-Assessment Result	Your Score
Listening Activity	I can get the right answer for the listening tasks.	10		
	I can grasp the general idea of the listening materials.	10		
	I can detect the details of the listening materials.	5		
	I can take notes when listening to classmates' presentations.	5		

Continued

Assessment Content	Assessment Standard	Total Score	Self-Assessment Result	Your Score
Role-play and Speaking Activity	I can use the skills and conduct the tasks required in this unit.	5		
	I can talk about the subject and its relevant information in this unit.	5		
	I can play well in the role-play.	10		
	I can express and present my ideas about the subject and its relevant information.	10		
Reading Activity	I can understand the main idea of the text.	5		
	I can use the words, phrases and sentence patterns in the text to finish the speaking exercises.	5		
Pronunciation	I can pronounce the new words correctly with a standard tone and rhythm.	10		
Fluency and Coherence	I can use a range of connectives and discourse markers to express my ideas with logic and coherence.	10		
Grammatical Range and Accuracy	I can use a mix of simple and complex grammatical structures, but with limited flexibility.	10		
Total		100		

Pre-exhibition Preparations

Learning Objectives

❖ Familiarize with words and expressions on pre-exhibition preparations.

❖ Learn to prepare for attending an exhibition.

❖ Master the skills concerning building a booth, airport security and inviting clients.

❖ Develop communication skills, cooperation skills and adaptability.

Warm-up

It often takes several months to get to an exhibition from preparation to launch, while the exhibition usually only lasts three to five days. It can be said that the site is the key to an exhibition, and pre-exhibition preparation is the top priority. From signing up for the exhibition to setting up the booth, from inviting clients to attending the exhibition, the arrangement and coordination of all kinds of work are in every detail. If not handled properly, any small matter may turn into a big problem, which will affect the effect of the entire exhibition.

Discuss the following questions in groups based on the background knowledge above.

1. What preparations should we do before attending an exhibition?

2. Have you visited any exhibition centers before? Share the information you have collected, such as the name of the exhibition, location, facilities, and so on.

Module 1   Entering the Exhibition and Security Check

Watch

Task 1   Watch the video and decide whether the following statements are *True* (T) or *False* (F).

1. George Parker is the manager of the company.   (   )

2. George Parker is very familiar with the security check.   (   )

3. There are three security inspections for the exhibitors to enter the venue.   (   )

4. There are a few security personnel patrolling the venue at any time.　　　　(　　)

5. They prepare some small gifts for customers.　　　　(　　)

Task 2　Fill in the blanks with the missing words based on the video.

1. There is always a sea of faces at _____ and we should wait patiently.

2. This will be a _____ trip for you.

3. Is the security _____ strict at the entrance of the Canton Fair?

4. Passports used abroad must be inspected by relevant international institutions and verified again by _____ police.

5. The first is a _____ initial examination, the second is through the security door, and the third is card swiping and facial testing.

6. It's so _____.

7. Have you brought your exhibition _____?

8. _____, exhibitor card and exit card are all here.

9. Our company's information, computer, _____ , business card, customer information form, small gifts, etc. are ready.

10. We must _____ the time when the samples finally enter the venue and withdraw from the exhibition.

Task 3　Watch the video again and choose the best answer to each question.

1. Where are George and Bill?

　　A. At the exhibition entrance　　　　B. At airport security

　　C. At boarding desk　　　　D. At the ticket office

2. How does George feel when he is waiting here?

　　A. Nervous　　　　B. Excited

　　C. Anxious　　　　D. Confident

3. They need to go through three security checks. The second is _____?

　　A. a manual initial examination

　　B. the security door

　　C. card swiping

　　D. facial testing

4. Exhibitors are required to take ID card, _____ and exit card.

　　A. passport

　　B. academic certificate

　　C. exhibitor card

　　D. employee's card

5. Which statement is true according to the dialogue?

A. George and Bill are patiently waiting for entering the exhibition.

B. George is afraid of the security inspection.

C. It's not important to determine the time when the samples finally enter the venue and withdraw from the exhibition.

D. George has forgotten to take the computer with him.

Task 4　Work in pairs and summarize the key points of the conversation. Then, try to retell the key points.

Learn

Learn the following *Words & Phrases* and *Sentence Drills*.

Words & Phrases

rewarding *adj.* 值得的，有报酬的

domestic *adj.* 国内的，家用的

security inspection 安检

ID card 身份证

exhibitor card 参展商证

exit card 撤展证

move on 上前

queue up 排队

card swiping and facial testing 刷卡与面部检测

Sentence Drills

1. With so many people queuing up here, we need to wait a little longer.

这么多人在这里排队，我们需要再等久一会儿了。

2. This will be a rewarding trip for you.

这次旅行会让你受益匪浅。

3. The Canton Fair implements a strict ID card inspection system.

广交会实行严格的身份证查验制度。

4. We need to go through three security checks. The first is a manual initial examination, the second is through the security door, and the third is card swiping and facial testing.

我们需要接受三道安检。第一次是人工初检，第二次是过安检门，第三次是刷卡与面部检测。

5. Our company's information, computer, digital camera, business card, customer information registration form, small gifts, etc. are ready.

我们公司的资料、计算机、数码相机、名片、客户信息登记表、小礼品等都准备好了。

6. Did the samples arrive yesterday?

样品是昨天运送到的吗？

7. We must determine the time when the samples finally enter the venue and withdraw from the exhibition.

我们一定要确定好样品最后进馆的时间和撤展的时间。

Role-play

Student A, an agent, initiates a conversation with a passenger, Student B, by stimulating the following dialogue.

❖ Student A gives the security check instruction to help Student B go through the entry.

❖ Student B gives a response to each instruction and goes through the entry smoothly.

   Some sentences are listed for your reference.

1. May I see your passport and ticket, please?

2. Please lay your bags flat on the conveyor belt and use the basket for small objects.

3. Please put all your metal objects such as coins, cellphones, chewing gum and cigarettes into the basket.

4. I'm sorry to tell you that flammable items cannot be take with you.

Speak

Read the following passage, take notes on Entry and Exit, and make a speech according to the passage.

How Much Do You Know about *Entry* and *Exit?*

1. Entry

   When foreigners come to China, overseas Chinese, residents of the Hong Kong and Macao Special Administrative Regions and compatriots from Taiwan(台湾同胞) travel to the mainland of the motherland, or Chinese citizens travel abroad and return, all of them must submit valid documents for examination at the designated Frontier Inspection Station (口岸边防检查站) which is composed of staff from public security, customs and health and quarantine, and foreign tourists must fill in an entry card and may enter the country only after the frontier inspection station has approved and stamped the inspection seal(验讫章).

   Passport and visa are the most basic requirements for entry and exit. With the development of international relations and tourism, many countries have signed mutual visa exemption agreements(互免签证协议).

2. Exit

Foreign travelers leaving the country

Foreign tourists should leave the country at the designated port within the period allowed by the visa. When leaving the country, you need to submit a valid passport or other valid documents to the border inspection station at the port for inspection, fill in the entry card and leave the country after stamping the exit inspection stamp.

Chinese travelers leaving the country

Chinese passengers leaving the country also must submit valid passports and visas to countries and regions to our country's border inspection stations. Before leaving the country, Chinese passengers must fill in the "Passenger Baggage Declaration Form" in duplicate(一式两份), and fill in the quantity, brand and specifications of important items such as watches, cameras, etc., so that they can use this form to check duty-free when returning to the customs.

Several things to know when entering or leaving the country:

(1) National prohibited items cannot be carried in and out of customs;

(2) The total price of duty-free goods cannot exceed RMB 8,000;

(3) Animals such as live poultry and wild animals are not allowed;

(4) Meat products, aquatic products, animal milk products, etc. are not allowed;

(5) Do not bring medicinal materials, fruits, eggs, seeds and other items;

(6) Foreign soil cannot be carried;

(7) If you are going abroad for the first time, understanding the above precautions will help you avoid unnecessary trouble and loss.

Module 2　Building a Booth

Watch

Task 1　Watch the video and decide whether the following statements are *True* (T) or *False* (F).

1. Baron Li has got the confirmation from China International Furniture Fair. 　(　)

2. SKY Furniture Trading Company will pay for the booth in time. 　(　)

3. X company, with rich experience, is the official booth contractor of the China International Furniture Fair. 　(　)

4. Workers should enter the Exhibition Center with Access Cards. 　(　)

5. On-site service is not available at the exhibition. 　(　)

Task 2　Fill in the blanks with the missing words based on the video.

1. Ivy Xie is reading the _____.

2. They got an ideal booth in the _____ the first row.

3. Ivy Xie called Christina Miller to enquire about _____.

4. Baron Li told Ivy Xie to pay the _____ in time.

5. X company as the official booth contractor has _____ in providing booth designing installation services.

6. The official booth contractor is selected with _____.

7. Booth contractors should submit their workers' name list and _____ one week earlier than the booth construction.

8. Workers should enter the Exhibition Center with _____.

9. Any booth contractor should obey the rules and _____ of the exhibition.

10. On-site service (现场服务) for _____ furniture or other facilities on the exhibition is available.

Task 3 **Watch the video and choose the best answer to each question.**

1. What is the spot of SKY Furniture Trading Company's booth on this exhibition?

    A. In the middle of the first row

    B. In the middle of the hall

    C. In the middle of the third row

    D. In the middle of the last row

2. How much should booth contractors pay for each card?

    A. ¥30

    B. ¥50

    C. $30

    D. $50

3. On-site service will be available at a surcharge of _____.

    A. 30%

    B. 20%

    C. 25%

    D. 35%

4. X company is selected as Christina's company's official booth contractor by its _____.

    A. low price

    B. rich experience

    C. last relationship

    D. warmness

Task 4   Work in groups and summarize the key points of the conversation. Then, try to retell the story in the video.

Learn

Learn the following *Words & Phrases* and *Sentence Drills*.

Words & Phrases

confirmation *n.*　确认，证实

contractor *n.*　承包商

exhibitor *n.*　参展商

installation *n.*　就任，安装

recommend *v.*　推荐

experience *n.*　经验

surcharge *n.*　附加费

accommodate *v.*　向……提供住处

be subject to surcharge　加收附加费

accommodation service　食宿服务

on-site service　现场服务

Access Cards　门禁卡

ID copies　身份证复印件

rules and regulations　规章制度

Sentence Drills

1. We get an ideal booth in the middle of the first row.
   我们得到了一个最佳位置，就在第一排的中间。

2. Of course, location is a top priority.
   当然，位置是首要考虑的问题。

3. I'm calling to confirm with you about the raw space design and installation of the booth.
   我致电与您确认有关光地设计和展位安装的信息。

4. You recommended your official booth contractor X company to exhibitors.
   您已向参展商推荐了贵方的官方展位承包商 X 公司。

5. Do we have to use this company to design and build our company's booth?
   我们必须请该公司来搭建展台吗？

6. They have rich experience in providing booth designing installation services.
   他们拥有非常丰富的展台设计与搭建的经验。

7. We have sent the rules and regulations of booth design and installation to exhibitors.
   我们已将展位设计和安装的规章制度发送给参展商。

8. The maximum height of the booth is the key point of the regulations.
   规定里面最重要的是展台的限高。

9. Speaking of fire safety, here are some detailed regulations.
   说到消防安全，这里有些详细规定。

Role-play

Martin is the marketing manager of Yacan Rice Co., Ltd. supplying rice products and Lily Chen is the sales manager of Saidol Group, a well-known international convention and exhibition company. Martin wants to apply for a booth for their rice products. They are talking about the booth design and installation. Work in pairs and role-play the conversation. Some sentences are listed for your reference.

1. What kind of booth would you like?

2. Do you have brochures(小册子)?

3. Do we have to use this official company to design and build our company's booth?

4. We have sent the rules and regulations of booth design and installation to exhibitors.

5. How can our workers enter the Center?

6. We'll abide by the rules and regulations strictly.

Speak

Read the passage below and discuss the solutions to get effective booth design. Then make a presentation on how to choose booth design.

How to Choose Booth Design

The exhibitors can hand over the design task to the designer to visualize the theme and content of the company's booth. Generally, designers will express their design plans through schematic diagrams of the layout (平面布局示意图), elevation design drawings of the booth (展位立面设计图), color renderings of the booth space, 3D demonstration animations or models, etc.

When designers carry out scheme design, exhibitors generally ask them to come up with several more plans. Since there is more than one way to solve the problem, different plans will have different uniqueness. Multiple plans help to explore ideas. With comparison and deliberation (深思熟虑) of multiple plans, we can find a satisfactory, novel (新颖的) and unique good plan. At the same time, we should be willing to give up the unnecessary parts and focus on the coordination (协调) and unity of function and form.

Booth design should be harmonious, concise, with clear focus and eye-catching signs, which can clearly express the theme and convey information.

Module 3   Inviting Clients

Watch

Task 1   Watch the video and decide whether the following statements are *True* (T) or *False* (F).

1. Ivy wants to build a new partnership with Steven.   (   )

2. Steven is willing to attend the exhibition.   (   )

3. SKY Furniture Trading Company has developed some kitchen appliances.　　　(　　)

4. Ivy gives details of the new products to Steven by phone.　　　(　　)

5. SKY Furniture Trading Company will have 3 booths at the Canton Fair.　　　(　　)

Task 2　Fill in the blanks with the missing words based on the video.

1. Hello, Ivy. I haven't seen you for a year. How is _____?

2. I'm calling to invite you to _____ Canton Fair, to be held in Guangzhou, from October 15 to 31, 2020.

3. Great. We _____ with your company last year, and the furniture sells well.

4. We received lots of _____ from the buyers .

5. Our company has developed some new furniture including _____.

6. Do you have the _____ of your new products?

7. I will send our _____ and information to your mailbox later.

8. This exhibition will provide _____ to everybody.

9. Wish you _____ of this exhibition.

10. Looking forward to seeing you _____.

Task 3　Watch the video again and choose the best answer to each question.

1. Why did Ivy call Steven?

　　A. Discussing attending an exhibition

　　B. Inviting Steven's company to the exhibition

　　C. Finding solutions to the sales problem

　　D. Inviting Steven to a party

2. The 128th Canton Fair will be held in Guangzhou, from _____.

　　A. October 15 to 31, 2020　　　　　　B. October 25 to 31, 2020

　　C. September 15 to 31, 2020　　　　　D. September 5 to 21, 2020

3. Ivy will send the product catalogue and information to _____.

　　A. SWC@163.com　　　　　　　　　B. SWC@126.com

　　C. FCD@126.com　　　　　　　　　　D. 45289@qq.com

4. Steven is satisfied with the furniture products because they received lots of _____ from the buyers .

　　A. orders　　　　　B. positive comments　　　　C. benefits　　　　D. subsidies(补贴)

5. The booth number is _____.

　　A. A-F-306,307　　　B. A-H-307,308　　　C. A-F-307,308　　　D. A-H-306,307

Task 4   Work in pairs and summarize the key points of the conversation. Then, try to retell the story in the video.

Learn the following *Words & Phrases* and *Sentence Drills*.

Words & Phrases

attend *v.* 参加

invitation *n.*   邀请

furniture *n.*   家具

reservation *n.*   预订

subsidy *n.*   补贴

catalogue *n.*   目录

demand *n.&v.*   需求，需要

venue *n.*   会场

discount *n.*   折扣

kitchen appliance   厨房用具

positive comment   好评

trade show   贸易展览会

Sentence Drills

1. Hello, this is South West company. Can I help you?

   您好，这是西南公司。我可以帮你吗？

2. I'm calling to invite you to the 128th Canton Fair, to be held in Guangzhou, from October 15 to 31, 2020.

   我谨邀请您参加 2020 年 10 月 15 日至 31 日

在广州举行的第 128 届广交会。

3. Our company has developed some new furniture including kitchen appliances.

   我们公司开发了一些新家具，包括厨房用具。

4. We made orders with your company last year, and the furniture sells well.

   去年我们向贵公司下了订单，家具的销量很好。

5. This exhibition will provide opportunities to everybody interested in SKY furniture and our new products and demand in the world market will be shown in the exhibition.

   这次展览将为每个对 SKY 家具感兴趣的人提供机会，我们的新产品以及世界市场对家具产品的需求情况将在展览中展示出来。

6. Wish you a part of this exhibition.

   希望您能参加这次展览。

7. It's worth going.

   很值得一去。

8. Hope to see you at the venue.

   希望能在会场见到你。

Role-play a conversation inviting clients to the exhibition. Student A, an exhibitor from Golden Elephant Toy Company in China, tries to invite student B to attend the China Import and Export Fair. Your company's booth is B-H-205. Student B, a former client, has established a cooperative relationship with SKY. They are talking on the phone. Work in pairs and role-play the conversation.

Some sentences are listed for your reference.

1. Hello. Can I speak to ...?

2. I'm calling to invite you to attend...

3. We made an order with you last year and the products sell well.

4. We have developed some new products and will offer a big discount for orders at the venue.

5. It's worth going.

6. Hope to see you at the venue.

Speak

Read the passage below and discuss what preparations exhibitors should make before the exhibition. Then, make a speech on why most exhibitors invite clients to visit their booth and how to invite clients to the booth successfully. Some words and phrases are listed for your reference.

1. in advance

2. target / potential visitor

3. face to face

4. patronize

5. join us in the 128th Canton Fair

6. establish a long term and good business relationship

7. Booth Number

8. at the venue

Inviting Clients

More and more exhibitors are setting the booths to be visited in advance. Therefore, if exhibitors do not prepare in advance and invite their target visitors (目标参观商), they may miss opportunities for cooperation. Inviting clients to the company's booth, exhibitors can communicate with customers face-to-face in more detail and strive for more cooperation opportunities. At the same time, making full use of the opportunity of the exhibition will save the time and a series of costs required to visit customers in different countries and regions. According to the survey, clients have four times more chances to patronize(光顾) the booths of companies that have sent invitations before the exhibition than to visit the booths of other companies. Therefore, inviting clients to participate in the exhibition is very important and effective.

Read the following invitation and learn how to invite clients successfully.

Invitation

Dear Sir / Madam,

SKY Furniture Trading Company sincerely invites you to join us in the 128th Canton Fair, to be held in Guangzhou, from October 15 to 31, 2020. You can visit http://www.cantonfairs.com/ for more information.

We are one of the most professional furniture manufacturers in China, our products covering various of furniture. We will show mainly the living room furniture, bedroom furniture, and some kitchen appliances in this exhibition. Please contact us if you have any interest in our products.

We are looking forward to establishing a long-term and good business relationship with your company.

Please be a part of this exhibition.

Booth Number: A-H-308,309.

It would be a great pleasure to meet you at the venue.

Sincerely,

Ivy Xie

Module 4   Further Exploration

Role-play

Student A, a salesgirl of Philips Lighting Company, is going to London to participate in Lux Live London (英国伦敦国际照明展览会) . It is her first time to go abroad and she is a little nervous. Student B, a colleague of student A, an experienced foreign trade staff, is sharing his knowledge and experience. One of the issues they talked about is the entry card.

❖ Student A tries to invent any details to finish the program.

❖ Student B tries to share tips based on the following passage.

Fill in the blanks based on the passage below, then use as many words and expressions in the passage as possible to make a conversation. Swap roles and practice again.

1. Entry card is also called _____.

2. We often should fill in the entry card with our _____, date of birth, nationality, _____ and other information consistent with _____.

3. Foreign visitors to the United States need to fill out a US _____ form in English and hand it to the airline after they get off the plane.

4. _____ is a white card that non-British people need to fill in before entering the UK.

5. A landing card is one of the _____ for entering the UK.

Entry Card

Entry card is usually called Arrival Card.

When traveling abroad, you are required to fill in an entry card. But due to the difference in language and format, many people do not know how to fill in the entry card correctly.

The flight attendant will issue entry cards before the plane lands, and there will also be entry cards in various languages on the counter before entering the airport, which can be taken and filled in by yourself. It is recommended to fill in the card on the plane to avoid waiting in line to fill in when entering customs; The card should be completed in English and the signature of the card should be the same as that on the passport.

The individual information including name, date of birth, nationality, occupation and others should be completely consistent with the passport. Length of stay, accommodation, the name of the hotel needs to be filled truthfully.

Foreign visitors to Australia need to fill in the entry card, both front and back of the card. Foreign visitors to the United States need to fill out a US customs declaration form in English and hand it to the airline after they get off the plane. If the whole family travels, one family only needs to fill out one form, but when it's a group trip with relatives or friends, each family needs to fill out his or her own. In England, it's specially called Landing Card. A landing card is a white card that non-British people need to fill in before entering the UK. It is one of the legal documents for entering the UK. It is necessary to pass through the customs. Passengers only need to fill in the white part, the blue box is filled in by British customs officers.

Module 5　Simulation Workshop

Step 1　Project Background

The SKY Furniture Trading Company will participate in the 2022 Milan International Office Furniture Expo in Italy. The sales manager Baron Li, the salesgirl Ivy Xie and the receptionist Serena Wang are talking about their preparations for attending the exhibition. Serena Wang is responsible for contacting the 2022 Milan International Office Furniture Expo to arrange the booth design and installation. Ivy Xie is responsible for inviting their clients. Henry Lau is a staffer from the 2022 Milan International Office Furniture Expo. Jessica Jung is a regular client of the SKY Furniture Trading Company.

Step 2　Suggested Preparations

1. Role Assignment

Build a team with 5 students. Then, decide roles for each team member who undertakes the corresponding task including exhibition task arrangement, communication with exhibition organizer, and inviting clients to visit booths.

2. Collect Information

Collect necessary information about the 2022 Milan International Office Furniture Expo and get ready for presentation.

3. Rehearse and Make Improvements

Have a rehearsal about the presentation and make improvements if necessary.

Step 3　Video Shooting

Shoot a video about the sum-up meeting. Hand in your video and your teacher will rank and award the top 3 videos.

❖ **Self-assessment**

Assess according to the following table and find out what progress you have made.

Learning Assessment

Assessment Content	Assessment Standard	Total Score	Self-Assessment Result	Your Score
Listening Activity	I can get the right answer for the listening tasks.	10		
	I can grasp the general idea of the listening materials.	10		
	I can detect the details of the listening materials.	5		
	I can take notes when listening to classmates' presentations.	5		
Role-play and Speaking Activity	I can use the skills and conduct the tasks required in this unit.	5		
	I can talk about the subject and its relevant information in this unit.	5		
	I can play well in the role-play.	10		
	I can express and present my ideas about the subject and its relevant information.	10		

Continued

Assessment Content	Assessment Standard	Total Score	Self-Assessment Result	Your Score
Reading Activity	I can understand the main idea of the text.	5		
	I can use the words, phrases and sentence patterns in the text to finish the speaking exercises.	5		
Pronunciation	I can pronounce the new words correctly with a standard tone and rhythm.	10		
Fluency and Coherence	I can use a range of connectives and discourse markers to express my ideas with logic and coherence.	10		
Grammatical Range and Accuracy	I can use a mix of simple and complex grammatical structures, but with limited flexibility.	10		
Total		100		

Visitors Reception

❖ Familiarize with words and expressions on reception, table manners, and seeing off.

❖ Learn to talk about reception, table manners and seeing off fluently in English.

❖ Master the listening skills concerning reception, table manners and seeing off.

❖ Develop basic etiquette in reception and business dining.

Warm-up

As the whole world becomes a global village, it is very important to know how to receive clients at an international exhibition. At the booth, you should give a precise and informative introduction to the products and the company to the visitors. Some questions concerning the information of prices, discounts, delivery time, etc. are repeatedly asked by the visitors. You are required to acquaint yourself with the products, reception skills and table manners when you are receiving the clients, as the first impression is essential to a successful business deal.

Discuss the following questions in pairs based on the background know ledge above.

1. Who do you think usually works on a stand at a trade fair (e.g. salespeople, marketing executives)?

2. What are the challenges of working on a stand at a trade show?

3. How much do you know about the differences between Chinese and Western table manners?

Module 1   Receiving Visitors at the Booth

Watch

Task 1   Watch the video and decide whether the following statements are *True* (T) or *False* (F).

1. George is interested in the chair at the showroom from ABC company.   (   )

2. George would like to have some coffee.   (   )

3. SKY Company is with over 20 years of history.   (   )

4. The best thing about the chair is cost-effective.   (   )

5. George and Ivy will meet again next morning.   (   )

Task 2   Fill in the blanks with the missing words based on the video.

1. Good morning. Welcome to _____.

2. There is _____ furniture showed at your booth and I like the design and style.

3. Er... I am _____.

4. 10 minutes will be OK and you are sure to find it _____.

5. Please _____. What would you like to drink, coffee, black tea or Coca Cola?

6. OK, let's _____.

7. We have been one of _____ of office furniture in China since 1998 and we supply file cabinets, office desks and chairs with US$ 18 million worth of products exported last year.

8. MacDonald and Huawei are among our _____.

9. We have various kinds of styles and sizes for you to choose from and can also offer _____.

10. They look _____.

Task 3   Watch the video again and choose the best answer to each question.

1. What is George exactly looking for?

   A. file cabinet   B. office desk   C. office chair   D. Not mentioned

2. What would George like to drink?

   A. black tea   B. coffee   C. Coca Cola   D. None

3. How much did SKY Furniture Trading Company export last year?

   A. US$ 80 million   B. US$ 18 billion   C. RMB¥80 million   D. RMB¥18 billion

4. Which one is not the specific function the chair has?

   A. It is adjustable.

   B. The wheels are very smooth.

   C. It makes the sitter keep in the right aligned position.

   D. It is with Ergonomic Backrests and Breathable Padded Seat.

5. Which statement is true according to the dialogue?

   A. Ivy managed to attract George's interest in some furniture of her company.

   B. The chair showed by Ivy is good but expensive.

   C. George is going to place an order with Ivy.

   D. The showroom is very spacious and beautiful.

Task 4　Work in pairs and summarize the key points of the conversation. Then, try to retell the story in the video.

Learn

Learn the following *Words & Phrases* and *Sentence Drills*.

Words & Phrases

exhibitor *n.*　展览商

booth/stand *n.*　展览摊位

worthwhile *adj.*　值得的

various *adj.*　多种多样的

distinguished *adj.*　尊贵的，著名的

catalog *n.*　产品目录

best-selling *adj.*　最畅销的

breathable *adj.*　透气的

file cabin　文件柜

Ergonomic Backrests.　符合人体工程学的靠背

Sentence Drills

◆ **Greeting clients at the booth**

1. Good morning. Welcome to our booth.

　早上好。欢迎光临我们的展位。

2. Hello, may I help you?/What can I do for you?

　您好，有什么可以帮到您吗？

3. Good morning, Mr. Parker. How are you? It's so nice to see you again. It has been a year since the last trade fair we met.

　早上好，帕克先生，您还好吗？很高兴又见到您！我们差不多一年未见面了！

◆ **Starting a conversation**

1. Thanks for your interest. Would you like to sit down and know more about our company and products?

　感谢您对我们的产品感兴趣。您愿意坐下来进一步了解我们的公司和产品吗？

2. What kind of products are you looking for?

　请问您在寻找哪类产品呢？

3. Here is our latest catalog. You may have a look at it and find if there is anything you are particularly interested in.

　这是我们最新的产品目录。您看看有没有特别感兴趣的产品。

4. Here is our catalogue and those on page 1 to 5 are all our best-selling products.

　这是我们的产品目录，第 1～5 页是我们的畅销产品。

Role-play

Task 1   Lee Wei is a stand staffer in HOMI MILANO supplying skincare products and William Hill is a visitor looking for hair-conditioners. Lee Wei tries to attract William's interest in his products. Work in pairs and role-play the conversation. Swap roles and practice again. Some sentences are listed for your reference.

1. Have you come across our products before?

2. If you have a spare moment, I'll give you a demonstration.

3. Who is your present supplier?

4. I hope we can conclude a deal for our mutual benefit.

5. Our hair-conditioners are famous for their high quality and reasonable prices.

Task 2   Think of a product you know well and role-play a conversation. Student A, a stand staffer, initiates a conversation with a visitor, Student B.

❖ Student A tries to invent any details to answer Student A's questions.

❖ Student B tries to raise some objections to buying Student A's product.

❖ Use as many words and expressions in the Sentence Drills as possible.

Swap roles and practice again. Some sentences are listed for your reference.

1. What's the USP (Unique Selling Proposition) of your product?

2. It is fancy, useless and expensive.

3. We offer a 3% discount for bulk purchases.

4. This is our freebies (赠品) and you can have a try.

5. When would be a good time to arrange an appointment?

Speak

Read the following advice for stand staffers. Match the collocations in bold (1–7) with the definitions (a–g) and **make a presentation** on **how to ensure success on your stand**.

a. Decide how likely someone is to buy a product/service.

b. Convince a person who has doubts about buying your product/service.

c. Answer questions, requests for information, etc.

d. Make people want to find out more about your product/service.

e. Have a polite and informal conversation.

f. Obtain information about customers.

g. Obtain a promise or guarantee that a customer will buy your product/service.

Want to ensure success on your stand?

Just remember the following seven tips.

1. Always be ready to **make small talk** with visitors to your stand. It's a great way into a sales conversation.

2. Always qualify **potential sales leads**.

3. **Deal with** customer **inquiries** politely but quickly. You don't want to leave other potential customers waiting!

4. Be prepared to **overcome objections** from potential customers confidently and effectively.

5. Try to **get a firm commitment to buy** while the customer is on the stand. Don't wait until the follow-up letter or email.

6. Remember that events are a great opportunity to **gather customer data**. Decide how you're going to do this before the event.

7. Finally, try to **generate interest in your product or service** in any way that you can. That's what events are for, after all!

Module 2 Having Dinner with Clients

Watch

Task 1 **Watch the video and decide whether the following statements are** *True* **(T) or** *False* **(F).**

1. David knows little of Chinese table manners.   (   )

2. David feels relaxed at the dinner.   (   )

3. David has found nothing particularly interests him.   (   )

4. Ivy would get an order from David the next day.   (   )

5. When having the long-stewed soup, we only eat the contents.   (   )

Task 2 **Fill in the blanks with the missing words based on the video.**

1. It's very kind of you to _____ us.

2. _____, I'm really a bit nervous now, as I know nothing of Chinese table manners.

3. It would be a shame to _____.

4. As for table manners, there is only one rule you must _____, that's to make yourself at home.

5. I hope the food we've ordered _____.

6. Thank you very much for such _____.

7. Thank you. It certainly looks very _____.

8. David, you will be leaving soon. Is your trip to this fair _____?

9. Yes, there has been a really wide range of good _____ and most of prices are reasonable.

10. Have you found anything that _____ interests you?

Task 3   Watch the video again and choose the best answer to each question.

1. Is David's trip to this fair fruitful?

　A. Yes, quite fruitful.

　B. No, he finds the prices are unreasonable.

　C. No, he finds the goods are quite inferior.

　D. Not mentioned.

2. What product is David interested in?

　A. Item AX6 and AX18

　B. Item AX6 and AX80

　C. Item AS6 and AS18

　D. Item AS6 and AS80

3. Which one is NOT true about the items that particularly interest David according to the dialogue?

　A. They are the latest designs.

　B. They are popular with women.

　C. They are popular with young consumers.

　D. They are original.

4. Which statement is true according to the dialogue?

　A. David had the long-stewed soup before.

　B. We have the long-stewed soup after the main dishes.

　C. We just drink the clear water and eat the contents when having "Lao Huo Liang Tang".

　D. Ivy and David are going to have good cooperation.

Task 4   Work in pairs and summarize the key points of the conversation. Then, try to retell the story in the video.

Learn

Learn the following *Words & Phrases* and *Sentence Drills*.

Words & Phrases

blunder *n.* 错误

observe *v.* 遵守

splendid *adj.* 丰盛的

fruitful *adj.* 成果丰硕的，富有成效的

original *adj.* 独创的

make oneself at home 不要拘束，别客气

suit one's taste 符合某人的口味

help oneself 随便吃，请自便

on display 展出

propose a toast 提议干杯

Sentence Drills

◆ **Taking an order**

1. What kind of meat would you like?

   请问您喜欢吃哪种肉？

2. What would you like to drink?

   请问您想喝点什么？

3. How do you like your steak done?

   请问您喜欢吃几成熟的牛排？

4. What kind of specialties do you have in the restaurant?

   请问你们有什么特色菜？

◆ **Expressing interest in establishing business relations**

1. We are willing to establish business relations for our mutual benefit.

   我们愿意基于互惠互利建立业务往来关系。

2. I do hope to have the opportunity for future cooperation.

   希望我们未来有机会合作。

3. May I know when can we have your order?

   请问我们什么时候能收到贵公司的订单？

4. I couldn't agree more.

   非常赞同。

◆ **Proposing a Toast**

1. May I propose a toast to our long friendly cooperation?

   我可以提议为我们的长期友好合作干杯吗？

2. To our cooperation and friendship!

   为我们的合作和友谊干杯！

3. May we succeed!

   祝我们成功！

Role-play

Role-play a conversation about having Morning Tea in Panxi Restaurant (Panxi Jiujia). Student A, an exhibitor from SKY Furniture Trading Company in China, is introducing Morning Tea to Student B, a client from KFC company in America.

❖ Student A tries to invent any details to answer Student A's questions.

❖ Student B tries to raise some questions about Guangzhou food.

❖ Use as many words and expressions in the Sentences Drill as possible.

Swap roles and practice again. Some sentences are listed for your reference.

1. As it goes, Guangzhou people eat everything in the sky and on the earth, except the plate and the stool.

2. Cantonese dim sum ranks the best in China.

3. The most typical ones: Shrimp Dumpling(虾饺), Steamed BBQ Pork Bun(叉烧包), Steamed Shaomai(烧卖), Jidi Congee(及第粥)，Chang Fen (Steamed Vermicelli Roll)(肠粉)，Shuang Pi Nai (Double-Layer Milk Custard)(双皮奶), etc.

4. What's the main ingredient?

5. How is it cooked?

6. When someone pours tea into your cup, you can tap the table three times with your bent forefingers and index fingers of your right hands, showing thanks to the pourer for the service and for being enough tea.

Speak

Read the passage below and discuss the differences between Chinese and Western table manners, then make a presentation on how to behave properly at dinner.

The Differences between Chinese and Western Table Manners

Different countries have their own unique (独一无二的) food culture. When it comes to table manners, they also vary (不同) from one country to another, so those who work in one country may not be acceptable in another. Chinese table manners differ greatly from those in western countries. The obvious difference is that the Chinese usually use chopsticks instead of knives or forks. In western countries, each one has his or her plate of food while in China several dishes are placed on the table and everyone shares. Another big difference is the order of serving (上菜). In China, the first dish is soup, followed by the staple food (主食), such as cooked rice, and then the last course is fruit to promote digestion. In western countries, the order of dishes is usually vegetables and soup, fruit, wine, staple food, and finally dessert and coffee.

One more main difference between Chinese and Western table manners is that Chinese tend to over-order food, for they will find it embarrassing (尴尬的) if all the food is eaten up; in contrast, it is considered bad manners in the West to leave one's food on the plate. During the dining, one of the things that surprises a Western visitor most is most of the Chinese hosts like to put food into the plates of their guests, which is a sign of friendliness and politeness, while it may discomfort (使……感到不舒服) the westerners as they have to eat the food even if they don't want to. Furthermore, it's important to remember to keep your elbows off the table and try to be quiet during eating in the West. However, people tend to talk with each other happily in Chinese dining.

In a word, when in Rome, do as the Romans do. To avoid embarrassment, figure out (弄明白) different table manners before you dine with your guests.

Module 3　Seeing off Clients

Watch

Task 1　Watch the video and decide whether the following statements are *True* (T) or *False* (F).

1. Ivy's company doesn't have a VIP car ready for George.　　　　　(　　)

2. George needs to leave his hotel at 14:00 tomorrow.　　　　　(　　)

3. George has his carry-on, a purse, and a large suitcase.　　　　　(　　)

4. Ivy is able to come in with George to say goodbye.　　　　　(　　)

5. Anyone can go into the departure area.　　　　　(　　)

Task 2　Fill in the blanks with the missing words based on the video.

1. Hi, Ivy, I remember we've just finished an order at the booth at _____.

2. It's been a _____ trip! Thank you for everything, Ivy.

3. For an international flight, it is required to check in two hours _____, so I need to leave my hotel at 14:00 tomorrow.

4. How much _____ will you bring?

5. Not too much, so a small but quite _____ car would be OK for you. May I know where your terminal is?

6. I need to _____ on the second level of the International Terminal since I am flying to London by Qatar Airways Company.

7. No, thank you. I know you are quite busy these days and have a lot of work to _____.

8. Thank you for your _____! It's a pity that I can't see you off at the airport.

9. So, the driver will pick you up at _____ at 14:00 o'clock tomorrow, right?

10. _____. Have a nice trip!

Task 3　Watch the video again and choose the best answer to each question.

1. Which one is correct according to the conversation?

　　A. David is from SKY Furniture Trading Company.　　B. David called Ivy.

　　C. David and Ivy concluded a deal at the Canton Fair.　　D. David will take a taxi to the airport.

2. For an international flight, how long does David Kilmer need to checkin in advance?

　　A. In two hours　　　B. In an hour　　　C. In half an hour　　　D. In 45 minutes

3. Where is David Kilmer's terminal?

   A. The second level of the International Terminal.

   B. The first floor of the International Terminal.

   C. The second floor of the International Terminal.

   D. The third level of the International Terminal.

4. What's David Kilmer's destination?

   A. Qatar   B. New York   C. Washington   D. London

5. When will the driver pick up David Kilmer at the hotel lobby tomorrow?

   A. 9 A.M.   B. 2 P.M.   C. 2 A.M.   D. 5 P.M.

Task 4   Work in pairs and summarize the key points of the conversation. Then, try to retell the story in the video.

Learn

Learn the following *Words & Phrases* and *Sentence Drills*.

Words & Phrases	**Sentence Drills**
rewarding *adj.* 有益的，值得的	◆ **Making phone calls to clients**
luggage *n.* 行李	1. Hello. Is David in? /Hello. Is David there, please?
carry-on *n.* 随身行李	您好。大卫，在吗？
suitcase *n.* 手提箱	2. May I speak to Mr. Gates?/Can I speak to Mr.
VIP car 贵宾车	Gates?
check in 办理登机手续	可以麻烦盖茨先生接电话吗？
the International Terminal 国际候机楼	3. Hello. Would you ask David to step to the
Qatar Airways 卡塔尔航空公司	phone, please?
the departure area 候机室，出境区	您好。可以找大卫接电话吗？
see off 为……送行，向……告别	4. Hello, I d like to talk to David.
in advance 提前，预先	您好，请让大卫接电话。
drop off 让……下车	◆ **Seeing off clients**
	1. I m calling to say goodbye.
	我打电话给是想跟您道别。
	2. When do you need to leave?
	您什么时候离开呢？

Role-play

Role-play a conversation about saying goodbye at the exhibition. Student A, an exhibitor from SKY Furniture Trading Company in China, tries to arrange a plan for student B to leave the booth. Student B, a client participating in the China Import and Export Fair, is going to leave the booth.

❖ Student A tries to invent any details to see off the client at the booth at the trade fair.

❖ Student B tries to give any information about your leaving plan to the exhibitor.

❖ Use as many words and expressions in the Sentence Drills as possible.

Swap roles and practice again. Some sentences are listed for your reference.

1. As you have a tight schedule, I will not take up more of your time.

2. I have to say goodbye to you. Have a nice trip!

3. Thank you so much for coming to our booth.

4. I hope we will see you again soon.

Speak

Read the passage below and discuss how to say goodbye to clients who do not have any interest in your products but keep talking to you. Then, make a presentation on how to behave properly to get out of a conversation. Some tips are listed for your reference.

1. Show respect to all visitors.

2. Do remember to keep polite all the time.

3. Even if you realize the visitors are not the target clients, you'd better not hand them off to another booth staffer.

4. Never ask any visitor to leave your booth directly.

How to Say Goodbye: 5 Ways for Booth Staffers to Disengage (解脱)

At the booth at the Canton fair, sometimes you will meet some difficult customers. For booth staffers, what are the effective ways to disengage? The following 5 ways are listed for your reference when you are dealing with difficult customers.

1. Give Thanks

When the visitors keep asking questions, but you know they are not the target customers, you can give thanks for their time to go around the booth. Giving thanks to them directly is one of the most effective ways to disengage. You can simply thank the customers for visiting the booth and tell them to feel free to look around the booth politely. And then you can step back or away from them.

2. The Card Trick

When you see the visitors going around the booth and asking the prices of the products casually, you can go to them and give them your business card or exchange business cards. In this way, business cards can be regarded as a signal to end the conversation. You can say it like this: "Here's my card, in case you or anyone you know may have an interest in our products, you can contact us at any time." or "I've enjoyed talking with you. Enjoy the rest of the show. "

3. Slow the Verbal Flow

Sometimes you happen to meet talkative visitors, and they are not interested in any product but they just keep talking about something else. In this case, you can recommend a booth with some kind of interest located near yours, and tell them they should go and check it out. For those who are still talking to you rather than go out to check, as soon as there is a pause in the conversation, you can ask them: "I wonder if you could do me a favor?" This will disrupt their verbal flow (滔滔不绝) and cause them to focus on you. Then you can say, "I've enjoyed talking with you. But I've got an appointment I need to get ready for, would that be OK?"

4. Create a Gesture

Sometimes it is not easy for you to disengage from a chatty visitor, and still, you have to maintain your politeness to keep listening, so you can create a subtle non-verbal gesture that your team knows and flash the gesture to get someone to help you out of the conversation.

Module 4　Further Exploration

Role-play

Student A, a journalist for a program from Guangzhou TV—*Share Your Story in Canton Trade Fair*, is interviewing student B, an exhibitor from SKY Furniture Trading Company about how to deal with unhappy customers in the trade fair.

❖ Student A tries to invent any details to finish the program.

❖ Student B tries to share stories based on the following passage.

❖ Use as many words and expressions in the passage below as possible.

Swap roles and practice again.

Dealing with Unhappy Customers

It's a big challenge to deal with difficult customers. However, if the situation can be handled well, the relationship may be able to be improved, and some further opportunities will be created. There are seven steps.

1. Adjust Your Mindset

You need to adjust your mindset by putting yourself into a customer service mindset as soon as you're aware that your client is unhappy. This is the first priority. That's to say you'd better set aside any feelings you might have that the situation isn't your fault, or that your client has made a mistake, or that he or she is giving you unfair criticism.

2. Listen Actively

The most important step in the whole of this process is listening actively to what your client or customer is saying. In this unhappy situation, he does want to be heard and to air his grievances(抱怨，苦水). You can start the conversation with a neutral statement, such as, "Let's go over what happened." or "Please tell me why you're upset."

3. Repeat Their Concerns

Once he takes the time to explain why he's upset, you should repeat his concerns so you're sure that you're addressing the right issue. You can use calm, objective wording. For example, "As I understand it, you are, quite rightly, upset because we didn't deliver the samples that we promised you last week."

4. Be Empathetic and Apologize

Once you're sure that you understand your client's concerns, be empathetic. You can show him you understand his feelings and use your body language to signal this understanding and empathy concerning his unhappiness.

5. Present a Solution

Once you know the problems of being unhappy with your client, you need to present him with a solution. By doing so, you can comfort him to some extent.

6. Take Actions and Follow-up

Once your clients and you agree on a solution, you need to take action immediately. Then you try to explain every step that you're going to take to fix the problem to your client.

7. Use the Feedback

Your last step is to reduce the risk of the situation happening again. The important part of the problem-solving way is to find the root of the problem, then you can make sure it's done immediately. Also, it is significant to ensure that you're managing complaints and giving feedback in a very effective way.

Module 5   Simulation Workshop

Step 1   Project Background

George Parker from ABC company visited the exhibition booth of SKY Furniture Trading Company at the Canton Fair and was very interested in some furniture. Therefore, George made an appointment that he would bring his boss Andy Hathaway here for further information the next morning. The sales manager Baron Li, the salesgirl Ivy Xie and the receptionist Serena Wang from SKY Furniture Trading Company are responsible for receiving Andy and George, and supposed to give a presentation about their company and featured products. They are discussing the coming reception task.

Step 2   Suggested Preparations

1. Role Assignment

   Build a team with 5 students. Then, decide roles for each team member who undertakes the corresponding task, such as, introducing ABC company or SKY Furniture Trading Company (including business scope, history, achievements, certificates, etc.), featured products or showroom.

2. Collect Information

   Collect necessary information and get ready for presentation.

3. Rehearse and Make Improvements

   Have a rehearsal about the presentation and make improvements if necessary.

Step 3   Video Shooting

Shoot a video about the whole reception of Andy and George. Hand in your video and your teacher will rank and award the top 3 videos.

❖ **Self assessment**

Make an assessment according to the following table and find out what progress you have made.

Learning Assessment

Assessment Content	Assessment Standard	Total Score	Self-Assessment Result	Your Score
Listening Activity	I can get the right answer for the listening tasks.	10		
	I can grasp the general idea of the listening materials.	10		
	I can detect the details of the listening materials.	5		
	I can take notes when listening to classmates' presentations.	5		
Role-play and Speaking Activity	I can use the skills and conduct the tasks required in this unit.	5		
	I can talk about the subject and its relevant information in this unit.	5		
	I can play well in the role-play.	10		
	I can express and present my ideas about the subject and its relevant information.	10		
Reading Activity	I can understand the main idea of the text.	5		
	I can use the words, phrases and sentence patterns in the text to finish the speaking exercises.	5		
Pronunciation	I can pronounce the new words correctly with a standard tone and rhythm.	10		
Fluency and Coherence	I can use a range of connectives and discourse markers to express my ideas with logic and coherence.	10		
Grammatical Range and Accuracy	I can use a mix of simple and complex grammatical structures, but with limited flexibility.	10		
Total		100		

Exhibits Presentation

Learning Objectives

❖ Familiarize with words and phrases on company's introduction, showroom's introduction and exhibits' introduction.

❖ Learn to talk about reception skills and communicative skills fluently.

❖ Master the listening skills concerning company's introduction, showroom's introduction and exhibits' introduction.

❖ Develop basic communicative knowledge about reception and interaction.

Warm-up

Exhibits presentation means the communication between the salespersons and clients. Usually, exhibitors are required to introduce some information about the company and the products to the clients with the help of the catalogue. When introducing the company, salesmen try to convince the clients of the financial strength and brand strength, the enterprise culture and the soft power of the company. By presenting the showroom and the exhibits, salesmen try to persuade the visitors to place orders and establish business relations in the long run. Exhibits presentation is essential to a successful business dealing.

Discuss the following questions in pairs.

1. When you introduce your company to your clients, what will you take into consideration?

2. When you invite a client to your showroom, what information do you need to prepare?

3. What are the choices of your exhibits when you try to persuade your clients to place an order?

Module 1　Introducing a Company

Task 1　Watch the video and decide whether the following statements are *True* (T) or *False* (F).

1. SKY Furniture Trading Company is located in Foshan, Guangdong province.　　　(　　)

2. SKY Furniture Trading Company aims at setting design, development, production, and sales service as a whole, building modern fashionable comfortable furniture.　　　(　　)

3. SKY Furniture Trading Company's unique people-oriented culture attracts and retains tens of thousands of customers.　　　(　　)

4. The products of SKY Furniture Trading Company carry only the social mainstream family-oriented furniture practical value.　　　(　　)

5. The company is able to leverage our buying power to maintain the demands of our loyal customers.　　　(　　)

Task 2　Fill in the blanks with the missing words based on the video.

1. It will be better for me to know more about it _____.

2. I have heard that Foshan _____ a "Chinese furniture manufacturing base".

3. Our company's unique people-oriented culture attracts and retains outstanding talents, providing quality service and driving product _____ for customers.

4. Later you will know you won't miss the bold and beautiful product _____ in showrooms.

5. Our products _____ the practical value and aesthetic value which the social mainstream family-oriented furniture calls for.

6. Our designers have always been _____ the good combination of art and fashion, nature and environmental protection, simplicity and amenity.

7. It is very good when you are taking the _____ concept into your production.

8. Fine _____ and beautiful designs have built up an enviable reputation, and high quality makes us a manufacturing leader in Foshan district.

9. And we pay special attention to _____ foreign fashion furniture design concept.

10. Yes, it's much better if your company is planning to _____ your overseas market.

Task 3　Watch the video again and choose the best answer to each question.

1. Where is Baron's company located?

    A. Dongguan, Guangdong province   B. Foshan, Guangdong province

    C. Shunde, Guangdong province   D. Guangzhou, Guangdong province

2. How many employers are there in Baron's company?

　　A. About 300　　　　B. About 400　　　　C. About 350　　　　D. About 380

3. What have the designers in Baron's company always been pursuing?

　　A. combination of art and fashion　　　B. combination of nature and environmental protection

　　C. simplicity and amenity　　　　　　　D. All of the above

4. Which one is NOT true about the products in Baron's company?

　　A. fine craftsmanship　　B. beautiful designs　　C. low prices　　D. high quality

5. What does Baron's company pay special attention to?

　　A. absorbing foreign fashion design concept　　B. absorbing the fashion design

　　C. attracting the foreign designer　　　　　　D. absorbing foreign fashion furniture design concept

Task 4　Work in pairs and summarize the key points of the conversation. Then, try to retell the key points.

Learn

Learn the following *Words & Phrases* and *Sentence Drills*.

Words & Phrases	Sentence Drills
unique *adj.* 独特的 concept *n.* 理念 environment-friendly *adj.* 有利环境的 enviable *adj.* 令人美慕的 reputation *n.* 声誉，名声 craftsmanship *n.* 工艺 aesthetic *adj.* 美学的 amenity *n.* 舒适，愉快 expand *v.* 扩张，增加 leverage *v.* 杠杆平衡 maintain *v.* 维持	1. Our products are endowed with the practical value and aesthetic value which the social mainstream family-oriented furniture calls for. 我们的产品被赋予了社会主流家用家具非常注重的实用性和美学价值。 2. Our company's unique people-oriented culture attracts and retains outstanding talents, providing quality service and driving product innovation for customers. 我们公司以人为本的独特企业文化吸引并留住了优秀的人才，为公司提供了高质量产品，不断创新，满足顾客的需求。 3. Our designers have always been pursuing a good combination of art and fashion, nature and environmental protection, simplicity and amenity. 我们设计师一贯追求艺术和时尚、自然和环保结合，注重产品的简洁性和舒适性。

4. And we pay special attention to absorbing foreign fashion furniture design concepts.

而且我们特别注重吸收外国时尚家具设计的理念。

5. And you can see that the Chinese modern furniture production technology is used to make our furniture series. Fine craftsmanship and beautiful designs have built up an enviable reputation, and high quality makes us a manufacturing leader in Foshan district.

可以看到，中国现代家具生产技术体现在我们家具系列产品中。产品绝佳的工艺和大方美观的设计为我们公司赢得好声誉，过硬的产品质量使我们公司成为佛山地区的销售冠军。

Role-play

Task 1 Student A, a sales manager in a furniture company, initiates a conversation with the agent, Student B.

❖ Student A makes an introduction to his/her company to help Students B know more about it.

❖ Student B responds to Student A's introduction appropriately.

Some sentences are listed for your reference.

1. I surf the Internet and just know a little about your company. Can you share more information about your company, please?

2. Here are the catalogues. You can look at them at first and then tell me the ones that leave you a deep impression.

3. Our company is located in Foshan, Guangdong province.

4. Our company pays special attention to absorb foreign fashion furniture design concept.

5. We take the environment-friendly concept into our production.

Task2 Work in pairs and role-play the conversation about introducing a furniture company's showroom. Student A, a sales manager, initiates a conversation with the agent, Student B.

❖ Student A makes an introduction to his/her company to help Students B know more about it.

❖ Student B responds to Student A's introduction fluently.

Swap roles and practice again. Some sentences are listed for your reference.

1. In this showroom, you can see the samples of our new products this year.

2. We have two types: cloth and leather, covering sofa series, chair series and bed series.

3. We can change the sizes and the colors of the products to meet your requirements.

Speak

Read the following passage, and work with your partner describing the furniture factory. Then make a presentation on how to introduce a factory to the visitors.

Tips for introducing a company

When introducing a company to clients, it's essential to give a full picture of the company to the clients, enhancing the chances of cooperation for each other. The following tips serve as reminders for you when you try to offer information about your company to potential clients.

1. Fully identify the factory.

2. Explain details of its history, business goals, company culture and mission.

3. Describe how the factory can benefit the potential clients.

4. Describe the products produced and how they are different from other manufacturers, as well as their competitive edge (竞争优势) .

5. Introduce the target markets and customers at home and abroad.

6. Introduce achievements in the past if there are any.

Module 2   Introducing a Showroom

Watch

Task 1   **Watch the video and decide whether the following statements are *True* (T) or *False* (F).**

1. The products of Baron's company are categorized into two types: cloth products and leather ones.   (   )

2. The clients can only see the uniqueness of the technology that combines the elements of stainless steel, steel and aluminum with the cloth and leather from the sofa series and leisure furniture series.   (   )

3. For the sofa series, there are 2-seat sofas and 3-seat sofas.   (   )

4. In George's market, a 3-seat sofa is very popular among the middle-aged couples to use at their homes while the young couples prefer the loveseats.   (   )

5. For the sofa series, the theme of the major products this year is "the light of the city" .   (   )

Task 2   **Fill in the blanks with the missing words based on the video.**

1. We _____ ourselves in the hearts of our customers by offering products that meet style expectations, price ranges and excellent quality.

2. Yes, when we design these types, we _____.

3. For the sofa series, the theme of the major products this year is "_____".

4. George, you can see sectional sofa(组合沙发) in front of us. It is named "_____". For the sectional sofa, we have corner, right arm chaise, 4-piece, U-shaped, and L-shaped.

5. Look, the color is white and gray, _____ cloth and leather with the metal element of stainless steel, steel and aluminum in an excellent way.

6. We have already _____ many orders from clients from North America, Middle East, South Africa, etc.

7. In that case, I'm thinking of placing a _____ order.

8. Usually, in many houses, an ottoman can be used as _____.

9. When I place an order, I would like to order _____ too because I am sure it will become popular in our market.

10. Here come the chair series: chair sets, dining chairs, _____ and folding chairs.

Task 3　Watch the video again and choose the best answer to each question.

1. What is the home culture which Baron's company strives to achieve?

　　A. A home of your dream with comfort.

　　B. A home of your dream with beauty and comfort.

　　C. A home of your dream with beauty and fashion.

　　D. A home of your dream with simplicity and comfort.

2. How many types of ottoman are there in the company?

　　A. four　　　　　B. one　　　　　C. two　　　　　D. five

3. Usually, in many houses, an ottoman can be used as a coffee table(茶几). According to Baron, where shall we put the ottoman to make it a fashion?

　　A. Both in the kitchen and in the bedroom　　B. In the kitchen

　　C. In the living-room　　　　　　　　　　　D. In the bedroom

4. For the bed series in Baron's company, there are four sizes, what are they?

　　A. Single, big, queen and king

　　B. Twin, full, queen and king

　　C. Single, full, queen and king

　　D. Twin, big, queen and king

5. There is one more showroom in the other part of the city. When will George go to visit it?

　　A. Next Monday　　　　　　　　　B. Tomorrow

　　C. Next Tuesday　　　　　　　　　D. Next Friday

Task 4   Work in pairs and summarize the key points of the conversation. Then, try to retell the story in the video.

Learn

Learn the following *Words & Phrases* and *Sentence Drills*.

Words & Phrases

showroom *n.*   展示厅，陈列室

combine *v.*   结合

stainless *adj.*   不锈钢的

leather *adj.*   皮革制的 *n.*   皮革，皮制品

steel *n.*   钢铁，钢制品 *adj.*   钢铁的，钢制的

ottoman *n.*   搁脚凳

aluminum *n.*   铝

slipcover *n.*   椅套

cushion *n.*   椅垫

fix *v.*   确定

storage ottoman   储物凳

ladderback chairs   梯背椅

folding chair   折叠椅

Sentence Drills

1. Our products are categorized into two types: cloth and leather products, including sofas, chairs and beds.
   我们的产品归为两类：布艺和皮质，包括沙发、椅和床。

2. You can find we combine the elements of stainless steel, steel and aluminum with cloth and leather in a very comfortable way.
   你可以看到我们的布艺沙发和皮革沙发在融合不锈钢、钢和铝时，有一种舒适大方的感觉。

3. For the sofa series, the theme of the major products this year is "the light of the city".
   我们的沙发系列产品，今年的主题是"城市之光"。

4. George, you can see sectional sofa in front of us. It is named "Sydney". For the sectional sofa, we have corner, right arm chaise, 4-piece, U-shaped, L-shaped.
   乔治，你现在看到的这套组合沙发，是名为"悉尼"的组合沙发。这套沙发包括转角、右扶手躺椅、4件套沙发、U形沙发、L形沙发。

5. Of course we have bed series. Usually, we have bed frames and headboard. There are four sizes: twin, full, queen and king.
   我们公司也有床系列产品。通常床系列包括床架和床头板。有四种尺寸：单人床、标准双人床、大双人床和加大双人床。

6. It's an ottoman. There are two types, one is storage ottoman and the other one is bench.
   这是搁脚凳。搁脚凳有两种类型，一种是储物凳，另一种是凳子。

Role-play

Role-play a conversation between a sales manager and an agent. Student A, a sales manager, initiates a conversation with an agent, Student B.

❖ Student A makes an introduction to the following 2-seat sofa to help Students B know more about it.

❖ Student B responds to Student A's introduction appropriately.

Swap roles and practice again. Some sentences are listed for your reference.

1. May I have more information about this sofa, please?

2. This is the 2-seat sofa. The material is cloth.

3. When we want to wash the slipcover of the sofa, what can we do?

4. The sofa can unpick and wash.

Speak

Read the following passage and picture. Then make a presentation on how to arrange a showroom to attract the clients to place an order.

The Interior Design of the Showroom

The purpose of the interior design of the showroom is intended to increase sales lead for a company. Understanding the market is essential for the interior design and the arrangement of the showroom. If the showroom is designed based on the market's needs, it will leave a forgettable impression on visitors. That is to say, to capture the attention and instill the imagination of visitors to conceive (酝酿) a lifestyle choice in sight is very important. A well-presented showroom can maximize sales lead well unexpectedly. The interior design of the showroom includes the delivery of all the furnishings (室内陈列品) and their arrangement in an aesthetically (美学地) and pleasing way as well as carefully planned final touches (修饰) and embellishments (装饰).

Module 3　Introducing Exhibits

Watch

Task 1　Watch the video and decide whether the following statements are *True* (T) or *False* (F).

1. Mr. Parker is not looking for the couch this time. 　　　　　　　　　　　(　)

2. Mr. Parker likes Chinese culture very much. 　　　　　　　　　　　　(　)

3. Mr. Li invites Mr. Parker to sit down and have a try. 　　　　　　　　(　)

4. The second new design looks like a flamingo seen from behind.   (   )

5. The second new design is quite different from the first one.   (   )

Task 2   Fill in the blanks with the missing words based on the video.

1. I _____ the concept of the series "City Lights" very much.

2. As for the office chairs, our company _____ two new designs this year.

3. This office chair is called Yoho, whose design _____ the concept of "_____" of traditional Chinese culture.

4. It takes its name from the Chinese meaning for _____ life.

5. This office chair is _____ a multi-functional chassis imported from Taiwan.

6. It has the same _____ and material as the former one.

7. The minimum _____ is 100 pieces, and the price changes according to your order.

8. Please contact me any time if you _____, so that I can send you the _____ as soon as possible.

Task 3   Watch the video again and choose the best answer to each question.

1. What is Mr. Parker looking for this time?

    A. Couches

    B. Office chairs and tables

    C. Shelves

    D. File cabinets

2. Which of the following statements is NOT correct?

    A. The chair design follows the human body's flexibility.

    B. The padded support in the lumbar zone fulfills a good posture and greater comfort.

    C. The multi-functional equipment of the chair is imported from Japan.

    D. Only the second design mentioned in the dialog is flamingo-shaped.

3. Which four colors do these two new chair designs come in?

    A. Black, blue, brown and white.

    B. Black, blue, red and white.

    C. Blue, gray, brown and red.

    D. Black, gray, blue and red.

4. How many pieces does Mr. Parker order?

    A. 100 pieces

    B. 50 pieces

    C. 200 pieces

    D. None of the above

Task 4　Work in pairs and summarize the key points of the conversation. Then, try to retell the story in the video.

Learn

Learn the following *Words & Phrases* and *Sentence Drills*.

<table>
<tr><td colspan="2">

Words & Phrases

flexibility *n.* 灵活性

postural *adj.* 姿势的，位置的

ergonomic *adj.* 人体工学的

headrest *n.* 头枕

armrest *n.* 扶手

adaptability *n.* 适应性

complement *v.* 补充

aerodynamic *adj.* 空气动力的

lumbar *n.* 腰椎

backrest *n.* 靠背

chassis *n.* 底盘

fabrics *n.* 面料

mold *v.* 浇铸

flamingo *n.* 火烈鸟

minimum *adj.* 最小的，最低的

quotation *n.* 报价

in all directions　全方位

seat depth　座深

one-step injection　一次性注塑

</td>
<td>

Sentence Drills

◆ **Introducing the exhibits**

1. This office chair is called Yoho, whose design originates from the concept of "harmony" of traditional Chinese culture.

   这款办公椅名为"悠活"，其设计灵感来源于中国传统文化"和"的理念。

2. It is designed to follow the human body's flexibility and every postural movement being perfectly ergonomic and highly functional.

   它的设计遵循人体的灵活性，每一个姿势动作都符合人体工程学和高度功能性。

3. The chair uses internationally popular color elements and environmentally friendly fabrics, and is molded by one-step injection.

   这款座椅采用国际流行的色彩元素和环保面料，一次性注塑成型。

◆ **Expressing interest and requirement**

1. I'm mainly looking for office chairs and tables.

   我主要想看一下办公座椅。

2. May I sit down and have a try?

   我可以坐下来试一下吗？

3. Can you show me the operation?

   你可以展示一下如何操作吗？

</td></tr>
</table>

Role-play

Lee Wei is a salesperson of HOMI MILANO supplying skincare products, and Jessica White is a visitor at the Canton Fair. Lee is introducing the hit product to Jessica. Work in pairs and role-play the conversation. Some sentences are listed for your reference.

1. Which product are you interested in?

2. Currently, there are three main product series in our company, including Absolute, Blanc Expert, and Men series.

3. Would you please tell me more about it?

4. It sells well in our country.

5. If you have booklets about the product, it would be nice.

Speak

Read the following passage about a product introduction at a trade fair and discuss with your partner about how to introduce the new product to the fair visitors effectively. Then make a presentation afterward and share it with your classmates.

Product Introduction at the Trade Fair

There are many advantages of doing product promotion during an exhibition. For one, you can easily get up close and personal with them which will allow you to build a business-to-consumer relationship. You can leverage(利用) on this as you encourage them to try out your products or even refer them to your friends. By getting to know your customers as well in the exhibition, you can market your products all you want without being limited to only a few words within a few seconds which is what an expensive advertisement usually allows. The only challenge is being able to do it right.

Pre-show marketing has made attendees eager to learn more about your product and see how it works. Hold product demonstrations throughout the show to increase buyer interest and generate qualified leads. Incorporate thoughtful ways to engage attendees while they learn more about the features and functions of your latest product. This will help drive excitement and make your product and brand more memorable.

The worse mistake you can do is not to be clear on the product that you're going to introduce. Many sellers often think that the more they describe, the easier it is for the customer to get an idea of what they are selling and what they can do. The truth is the longer your introduction is, the less interested the customers get. Also, there are instances when techie individuals (技术人员) already have researched the product before checking out what you have to offer. In this case, extensive product descriptions can just remain on the fine print. However, don't forget to emphasize the benefits and the selling points. These will win your products some brownie points (加分) with the consumers.

Module 4　Further Exploration

Role-play

Student A, an intern from ABC Vocational College, is interviewing student B, an experienced exhibitor from SKY Furniture Trading Company about how to publicize a company at the exhibition.

❖ Student A tries to invent any details to finish the program.

❖ Student B tries to share the skills based on the following passage.

❖ Use as many words and expressions in the following passage as possible.

Swap roles and practice again.

How to Publicize a Company at the Exhibition

Participating in an exhibition is a great opportunity to introduce your company, promote its image and make known about your products. Before and during an exhibition, good preparations should be made in booth layout and publicity to ensure the best effect.

1. Make Full Preparations for the Exhibition

(1) Set objectives. List all the objectives we are expected to achieve in advance so that we have a clear mind about what are they and how to do them.

(2) Clarify work items. To achieve the above objectives, we need to clarify work items and complete each specific item.

(3) Do a good job in the fund budget. Make an elaborate fund budget beforehand to avoid unnecessary cost overrun.

2. Booth Design, Novel and Unique

To make your company impressive, the layout of the booth and the display of exhibits should reflect the uniqueness of your company and its products.

(1) Insist on being different. Combining with the characteristics of the enterprise and its products, the layout of the booth must be innovative and distinctive.

(2) Do well in advertising highlights. Strive to create 1−2 bright spots in booth layout, outdoor advertising, soft advertising, etc.

3. Three-dimensional and All-round Publicity

To achieve the Omni-directional publicity, a good image for the enterprise must be set up with the following tips.

(1) Prepare publicity materials. All the materials should be fully prepared beforehand.

(2) Send out invitations. It's necessary to send invitations in advance to all customers, agents, news media, authorities, etc. and essential to get in touch with news media to propagandize your

company by soft advertising.

(3) Coordinate relationships with all parties. To establish a good relationship with the leaders of the local, provincial and national organizing committee, and try to win their support and help.

(4) Create a pleasing atmosphere. In large-scale exhibitions, the drum band, song and dance performances, the Suona team, etc. can be performed timely to attract visitors' attention.

(5) Make good use of the off-site display. To cooperate with the inner exhibition, outdoor displays must be arranged in various forms and different places.

(6) Receive visitors attentively and heartily. Customer reception is important to the corporate image. Therefore, the staff should obey "four dos" and "seven don'ts". That is, to wear your brand name; be full of enthusiasm; use potential customers' names; arrange trained staff to receive visitors. Don't sit in the booth; don't read; don't make calls; don't group with others; don't eat in the booth; don't chat with other booth staff; don't judge customers by their appearance.

Module 5   Simulation Workshop

Step 1   Project Background

SKY Furniture Trading Company will attend the next Guangzhou Furniture Fair and a team of 5 members will be formed to prepare the furniture exhibition. The team members include George Gao, a new comer, Andy Hathaway, the boss, Baron Li, a sales manager, Ivy Xie, a salesgirl, and Serene Zhang, a receptionist. They are having a meeting to talk about the preparation for the exhibition, booth design, products layout, customers reception, furniture the introduction, and company publicity.

Step 2   Suggested Preparations

1. Roles Assignment

Build a team with 5 students. Then, decide roles for each team member who undertakes the corresponding task, such as, introducing the preparation of the exhibition, booth design, the display of products, publicity of the company, etc.

2. Collect Information

Collect necessary information and get ready for presentation.

3. Rehearse and Make Improvements

Have a rehearsal about the presentation and make improvements if necessary.

Step 3   Video Shooting

Shoot a video about the sum-up meeting. Hand in your video and your teacher will rank and award the top 3 videos.

❖ **Self-assessment**

Assess according to the following table and find out what progress you have made.

Learning Assessment

Assessment Content	Assessment Standard	Total Score	Self-Assessment Result	Your Score
Listening Activity	I can get the right answer for the listening tasks.	10		
	I can grasp the general idea of the listening materials.	10		
	I can detect the details of the listening materials.	5		
	I can take notes when listening to classmates' presentations.	5		
Role-play and Speaking Activity	I can use the skills and conduct the tasks required in this unit.	5		
	I can talk about the subject and its relevant information in this unit.	5		
	I can play well in the role-play.	10		
	I can express and present my ideas about the subject and its relevant information.	10		
Reading Activity	I can understand the main idea of the text.	5		
	I can use the words, phrases and sentence patterns in the text to finish the speaking exercises.	5		
Pronunciation	I can pronounce the new words correctly with a standard tone and rhythm.	10		
Fluency and Coherence	I can use a range of connectives and discourse markers to express my ideas with logic and coherence.	10		
Grammatical Range and Accuracy	I can use a mix of simple and complex grammatical structures, but with limited flexibility.	10		
Total		100		

Business Negotiation

Learning Objectives

❖ Familiarize with words and expressions on pricing, payment, shipment, packing, insurance and contract.

❖ Learn to talk with the client about pricing, payment, shipment, packing, insurance and contract.

❖ Master the basic skills and strategies for negotiation.

❖ Develop a better understanding of commonly-used international trade practices.

Warm-up

In business, almost every transaction involves a certain amount of negotiation. Business negotiation can be interpreted as encounters between two or more companies to reach agreements to achieve mutual economic benefits. When one is in business, negotiating the best possible deals is a high priority. Successful negotiation can bring profits to the company while poor negotiation can cripple a company just as quickly as losing key customers.

Discuss the following questions in pairs based on the background knowledge above.

1. What are the goals in business negotiation?

2. Can you list the factors that influence the buying decisions (e.g. product, service, price, performance) to achieve the goal?

3. What subjects or issues would often be included in the business negotiation? Which is the most sensitive one?

4. What will you do to get the upper hand in a price negotiation?

Module 1　Negotiating the Price

Watch

Task 1　Watch the video and decide whether the following statements are *True* (T) or *False* (F).

1. Andy is interested in the coffee table CT25088. ( )

2. The first price Baron offered is US$20 FOB Shenzhen, or US$24 CIF Liverpool per piece. ( )

3. Andy insists on a 15% discount and refuses to make any concession. ( )

4. The coffee tables' sales volume is falling greatly because of the economic crisis. ( )

5. Baron will give Andy the final decision after he reports to the head office. ( )

Task 2　Fill in the blanks with the missing words based on the video.

1. I'm glad to _____ you for the coffee table CT25008.

2. You can't be serious. That's too _____.

3. Our products are of high quality and in the _____.

4. Frankly speaking, we've already given you our _____ price because we are sincere in our cooperation.

5. That's an _____, but we are hoping for 15% off.

6. Wow, you are driving _____.

7. What we've offered is a fair price. You know, we have got _____ to cover.

8. The problem is that at your price, it's really difficult for us to _____ and open our market in our country.

9. Let's _____ and call it 12% off to conclude the business.

10. Great! I am glad we finally _____ the price.

Task 3　Watch the video again and choose the best answer to each question.

1. What item's price is Andy inquiring about?

　A. coffee table CT25088　　　　　　B. end table CT25088

　C. coffee table CT25008　　　　　　D. end table CT25008

2. What's the price for the item Andy and Baron are discussing about?

　A. US$24 CIF Liverpool　　　　　　B. US$24 FOB Shenzhen

　C. US$20 CIF Liverpool　　　　　　D. US$12 FOB Shenzhen

3. Which one of the following is NOT the reason why the item is selling at such a price?

　A. It's well-designed.　　　　　　　B. It is of high quality.

　C. The material is environmentally friendly.　　D. The material is getting more and more expensive.

4. How much discount do Baron and Andy finally agree on?

    A. 10%   B. 12%   C. 15%   D. 20%

5. Which statement is true according to the dialogue?

    A. The pandemic is influencing the sales volume of the coffee table in Andy's country.

    B. Andy is expecting Baron's reply the day after tomorrow.

    C. The coffee table is selling well in Andy's country.

    D. Baron promises Andy to give him a 15% discount.

Task 4　**Work in pairs and summarize the key points of the conversation. Then, try to retell the story in the video.**

Learn

Learn the following *Words & Phrases* and *Sentence Drills*.

Words & Phrases	Sentence Drills
sincere *adj.*　真诚的	◆ **Inquiring about the price**
delicate *adj.*　种类，多样化	1. How much are you selling it for?
cooperation *n.*　合作	你打算卖多少钱?
quote *v.*　报价	2. What's the price for it?
quotation *n.*　报价	这个价格多少?
flexible *adj.*　灵活的	3. Could you give us some idea about your
pandemic *n.*　流行病	prices?
offer *n.*　出价	能跟我们说一下你们的价格吗?
discount *n.*　折扣	4. I've come to hear about your quotation for...
way too　太	我是来听你们对……的报价的。
trim off　去掉，修剪	◆ **Negotiating the price**
drive a hard bargain　讨价还价	1. Can you lower the price a little?
rock-bottom price　最低价，底价	你能把价格降低一点吗?
sales volume　销售量	2. That's an attractive offer, but we are hoping for...
split the difference　折中	这个报价很有吸引力，但我们希望……
fixed costs　固定成本	3. Let's split the difference and call it...
make a profit　盈利	我们各让一点，……成交。
FOB　离岸价	4. How about we meet each other halfway and
CIF　到岸价	conclude the business?
	我们各让一半成交怎么样?

Role-play

A Canadian company makes a counteroffer after it receives an offer of sportswear article 280 from Anta Clothing Company. Then the two parties hold further discussions on the price issue. Work in pairs and role-play the conversation. Swap roles and practice again. Some sentences are listed for your reference.

1. How much are you selling it for?

2. I am afraid the price is working against us.

3. I hope you can reduce the price by ... (10%, $10 per piece, etc.).

4. Our sportswear is famous for ... (soft texture, high quality, reasonable price, delicate design, etc.)

Speak

Read the passage below and discuss the effective price negotiation strategies, then make a presentation on it.

How to Negotiate the Price—While Keeping Customers Happy

No matter how reasonable or competitive you believe your pricing is, it's still possible for you to run into some customers who want a better deal. It can be tempting to play hardball, or in some cases, simply walk away. However, if you can negotiate a win-win solution, you'll not only preserve your interests but also possibly build a long-lasting relationship with your customer.

The followings are some tips for negotiating a win-win solution that can keep both you and your customer happy.

1. Ask questions.

Spend some time asking questions and listening rather than just repeat your bottom line over and over again. In this way, you can get to the heart of what your customer is looking for. Find out their true priorities (优先考虑的事) and you may figure out how you can provide something they care about.

2. Avoid negotiating the price alone.

If your customers aren't opening up about their needs, think about whatever value you can add that doesn't involve price, and get prepared to utilize these as variables in the negotiation. As you discuss value-added propositions from your perspective, you may trigger (触发) the customer to show what they're really looking for. When you understand your customers' agenda and the ways you can add value beyond price, you may find your win-win (双赢).

3. Make smart concessions (让步).

Consider giving a little by offering things that your customer values highly, but that have a low incremental cost (增量成本) for your business. For example, some timelines can be adjusted so the work is done faster than anticipated. That can feel like a great bonus (红利). Or there is something in the payment schedule that can be adjusted. What is universally acknowledged is that if your customer is in negotiation mode, they probably want to walk away with something.

4. Be transparent about your dual needs.

Conversations are more productive when both sides are open. Rather than standing firm with no further explanation, try to have a discussion involving both their needs and your needs. Explain what the cost involves and why it is what it is. If your price is higher than others, explain to the customer why it is and what they are getting for the additional cost. Make sure they understand that you value the relationship and want to meet their needs, but that you also have a business to run and therefore can only go so far.

5. Always put the relationship first.

Demonstrate a kind of care that goes beyond the immediate deal. Concentrate on how you can satisfy your customer in the long run and your customer might place trust in you. If the customer knows you care about them and about the work you are doing, you could earn a customer for life.

Keep in mind that a negotiation is a chance to listen and to be heard, to show and earn respect and to develop a solid (牢固的) and lasting relationship with your clients.

Module 2　Negotiating the Payment

Watch

Task 1　Watch the video and decide whether the following statements are *True* (T) or *False* (F).

1. Baron accepts payment by L/C. （　　）

2. Andy thinks that payment by L/C also works to his advantage. （　　）

3. In Andy's case, a letter of credit would reduce the cost of his imports. （　　）

4. For Baron, payment by L/C can provide him a guarantee. （　　）

5. If Andy doesn't want the shipment to be delayed, he'd better make sure that the L/C reaches Baron 30 days before the date of delivery. （　　）

Task 2　Fill in the blanks with the missing words based on the video.

1. Since the problems of price and quantity have been settled, now let's talk about the _____.

2. The only mode of payment we can accept is payment via a _____ L/C payable against the presentation of shipment documents.

3. I'm afraid not. We don't want to _____ losing money.

4. That will not only _____ our money but also increase our costs.

5. For future _____ we may allow other ways of payment such as D/P, but not now.

6. In your case, I think you can consult your bank and see if they agree to reduce the required _____ to a minimum.

7. As you know, an irrevocable L/C provides us an additional protection of _____ .

8. This is also the usual practice _____ internationally.

9. L/C at sight is what we request from all our customers for such _____, especially with our new customers.

10. Do you have any other _____ for the L/C?

Task 3 **Watch the video again and choose the best answer to each question.**

1. What are they negotiating?

   A. L/C

   B. price

   C. terms of payment

   D. quantity

2. What mode of payment does Baron accept?

   A. L/C   B. D/A   C. D/P   D. cash

3. Which one of the following is NOT the reason why Andy suggests other ways of payment instead of accepting L/C directly?

   A. Payment by L/C will increase his cost.

   B. Payment by L/C will tie up his money.

   C. There are bank charges and fix expenses in opening an L/C.

   D. He can reduce the required margin to a minimum with other ways of payment.

4. Why does Baron insist on payment by L/C?

   A. L/C is the only way of payment allowed for exports internationally.

   B. Payment by L/C gives him a guarantee from the bank for the order.

   C. Payment by L/C will help him make more money.

   D. Not mentioned.

5. When should the L/C reach Baron?

   A. 13 days after the date of delivery.

   B. 30 days after the date of delivery.

   C. 13 days before the date of delivery.

   D. 30 days before the date of delivery.

Task 4   Work in pairs and summarize the key points of the conversation. Then, try to retell the story in the video.

Learn

Learn the following *Words & Phrases* and *Sentence Drills*.

Words & Phrases

confirmed *adj.*　保兑的

irrevocable *adj.*　不可撤销的

dealing *n.*　交易

margin *n.*　保证金

guarantee *v.*　保证，担保

adopt *v.*　采取

commodity *n.*　商品

consult *v.*　商议，咨询

balance *n.*　余额

minimum *n.*　最小值

delivery *n.*　交货，交付

terms of payment　付款方式

run the risk of　冒……的风险

tie up　占用

make an exception　破例

D/A　承兑交单

D/P　付款交单

L/C　信用证

documentary credit　跟单信用证

Sentence Drills

◆ **Asking and stating terms of payment**

1. What mode of payment do you accept?
   你们接受哪种付款方式？

2. Which way of payment do you prefer?
   你们喜欢哪种付款方式？

3. Our standard terms of payment are...
   我们标准付款方式是……

4. We would like/ prefer payment by ...
   我们偏向……的付款方式。

◆ **Refusing other ways of payment**

1. I can't be of any help in this respect.
   在这方面我帮不了什么忙。

2. As our usual practice, we can only accept...
   一般来说，我们只接受……

3. I'm sorry, we insist on payment by ...
   很抱歉，我们坚持……的付款方式。

4. I'm afraid I can't promise you even that.
   即使那样，恐怕我也不能答应你。

◆ **Persuading others to accept your terms of payment**

1. L/C can guarantee your in-time receipt of the order.
   信用证可以保证你方及时收到订单。

2. I think you can consult the bank and ask them to/ see if they agree to/ can reduce the required deposit/ margin to a minimum.
   我觉得你可以和银行商量一下，看他们是否同意把押金/保证金减到最低限度。

3. As you know, an L/C gives the exporter an additional protection of the banker's guarantee.
   你知道，信用证给出口商增加了银行的担保。

Role-play

At the Canton Fair, after agreeing on the price and quantity, Shillton Household Equipment Company is having a further face-to-face discussion with Haier Group on the payment of a washing machines. Haier Group insists on the payment by L/C while Shillton Household Equipment Company suggests D/A or D/P. Work in pairs and role-play the conversation. Swap roles and practice again. Some sentences are listed for your reference.

1. What mode of payment do you accept?

2. Our usual payment terms are...

3. I can't be of any help in this respect.

4. As you know, an L/C gives the exporter an additional protection of the banker's guarantee.

5. I think you can consult the bank and ask them to reduce the required margin to a minimum.

Speak

Read the passage below and do more research on the different payment methods in international trade. Then make a comparison of them, rank all the payment methods in terms of security for the seller and the buyer respectively, and finally make a presentation on it.

The 4 Most Common Payment Methods in International Trade

Besides price, the payment method is another important factor that buyers and sellers would consider before signing a contract. Frankly, it is not easy for a buyer and a seller to agree on the same payment terms, since the terms that are favourable to the buyer are often not the case for the seller. Here we'll list the four types of payment methods widely used internationally.

1. Cash in Advance

It is a type of payment where the buyer pays the seller upfront before the shipment of the goods. The two most frequently used payment options for this method are wire transfers and credit cards. Obviously, with this method, the seller is protected from buyers who may not honor the terms of the contract and decide not to pay. In other words, this method is not advantageous (有利的) to the buyer as the buyer will face the risk of receiving goods that don't meet the quality agreed in the contract, or even not receiving the goods altogether.

2. Letter of Credit

A letter of credit is a letter from a bank guaranteeing that a buyer's payment to a seller will be received on time and for the correct amount. If the buyer refuses or fails to pay for the goods purchased (购买), the bank will be required to cover the full or remaining amount of the purchase. To issue a letter of credit, the bank would require some form of securities or cash as collateral and charge a service fee, typically as a percentage of the value of the L/C. There are several types of L/C, such as irrevocable, revocable, and confirmed L/C.

L/C is one of the most commonly-used payment methods in the import and export industry as it minimizes risk for both the buyer and the seller. It not only protects the buyer since payment is only required after the shipment and delivery of the goods but also protects the seller since the bank is guaranteeing the payment as well as conducting a verification (核实) process to ensure the legitimacy (合法) of the buyer. However, compared with other payment methods, letter of credit is more expensive. As for the reliability of the L/C, it depends on the reputation (名声) of the buyer's bank.

3. Documentary Collections (D/C)

Documentary Collections is a payment term where the seller relies on the seller's bank (remitting bank) (托收行) to collect payment from the buyer. The seller would send the document to the remitting bank, which is forwarded (转递) to the buyer's bank (collecting bank) (代收行) together with the instructions for payment. The document is called a bill of exchange (draft) which requires the buyer to pay the face amount either at sight or on a specified future date. The buyer would then send the fund to the collecting bank, which is transferred to the seller through the remitting bank in exchange for those documents. There are two types of D/Cs, document against Payment (D/P) and document against Acceptance (D/A).

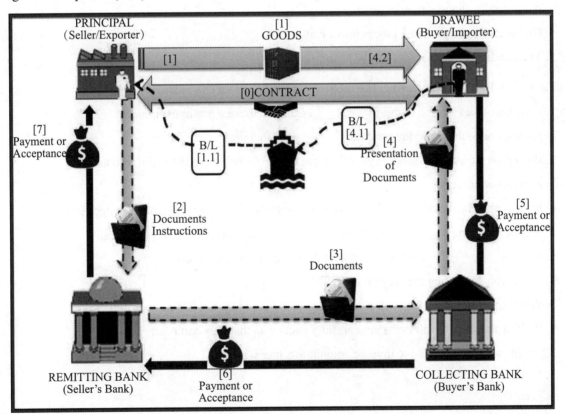

Compared with L/C, it's cheaper and less complicated. Since the buyer is not obligated to pay for goods before shipment, this payment method is more favourable to the buyer. However, it's riskier for the seller since there is no verification process, considering that the bank does not guarantee payment.

4. Open Account

Open account is a transaction (交易)where the seller is only paid typically in 30, 60, or 90 days, after the shipment and delivery of goods to the buyer. Sellers accepting open account payment methods can use export credit insurance if they seek additional security. This method is by far the most secure for the buyer as payment is not obligatory (强制的) until they receive the goods.

Module 3　Negotiating Other Terms

Watch

Task 1　Watch the video and decide whether the following statements are _True_ (T) or _False_ (F).

1. Baron agrees to make prompt shipment. 　　　　　　　　　　　　　　（　　）

2. The liner space for Europe had been fully booked up to the end of next month. （　　）

3. Andy finally chooses transshipment. 　　　　　　　　　　　　　　　（　　）

4. Coffee tables are packed 2 pieces into a carton. 　　　　　　　　　　　（　　）

5. The goods have been insured in W.A. terms. 　　　　　　　　　　　　（　　）

Task 2　Fill in the blanks with the missing words based on the video.

1. Now Baron, let's come to the _____. Can you make a prompt shipment?

2. As you know, those products are our _____ this year.

3. But I promise you that these days we'll have workers working in three shifts so as to _____ against your orders.

4. Is there any chance of _____ to be allowed? Or do you have any other suggestions?

5. We are operating a _____ from Guangzhou, Shanghai to Europe sea routes.

6. Besides, _____ are used to protect the goods against the press.

7. Could you strengthen the cartons with _____?

8. We all know strong packing will protect the goods against any possible damage during _____.

9. We'll make sure that all items are carefully packed so that they can reach you _____.

10. Premium will be added to invoice amount together with _____.

Task 3   **Watch the video again and choose the best answer to each question.**

1. Which of the following is the reason that prompt shipment is impossible for Baron?

   A. The liner space for Europe had been fully booked up until the end of next month.

   B. There are not sufficient products in stock right now.

   C. Transshipment is not available.

   D. Not mentioned.

2. According to Baron, why is transshipment a bad option?

   A. It increases the expenses.   B. It may result in delayed arrival.

   C. It increases the risks of damage.   D. All of the above.

3. What kind of shipment does Andy choose in the end?

   A. Direct shipment   B. Prompt shipment   C. Transshipment   D. Container vessel

4. How many pieces of coffee tables are packed into a carton?

   A. 2   B. 4   C. 8   D. 12

5. What kind of insurance does Baron provide for the consignment?

   A. F.P.A.   B. W.P.A.   C. F.W.A.   D. All risks

Task 4   **Work in pairs and summarize the key points of the conversation. Then, try to retell the story in the video.**

Learn the following *Words & Phrases* and *Sentence Drills*.

Words & Phrases

shift *n.* 轮班	strap *n.* 打包带
transshipment *n.* 转运	transit *n.* 运输
option *n.* 选择	insurance *n.* 保险
expense *n.* 开支	premium *n.* 保险费
costly *adj.* 昂贵的	liner space 班轮舱位
vessel *n.* 船	best sellers 热销商品
lot *n.* 份额，（货物的）批次	container service 货柜运输
carton *n.* 纸板箱	foam plastics 泡沫塑料
sufficient *adj.* 足够的	last resort 最后手段
consignment *n.* 托运的货物	in good condition 状况良好
invoice *n.* 发票	freight charges 运费
	prompt shipment 即期装运

effect shipment　装运

W.A./W.P.A.　水渍险

F.P.A. (Free from Particular Average) 平安险

all risks　综合险

the risk of breakage　破碎险

risks of damage　毁损风险

insurance against war risk　战争险

insurance against rain and fresh water　淡水雨淋险

insurance against TPND　偷盗、提货不着险

insurance against breakage　破碎险

insurance against leakage　渗漏险

different types of packing　不同包装类型

wooden case—for instruments, parts, medicines
木箱——用于仪器、零配件、药品

carton—for plastics, milk power, textiles, sundry goods
纸板箱——用于塑料制品、奶制品、纺织品、干果制品、水果

Sentence Drills

◆ Shipment

1. When and how are you going to ship our goods?

   你们打算什么时候、用什么方式装运我们的货物？

2. There would be no enough space for a full cargo. You should allow partial shipment.

   没有足够的空间装满货物，你们应该允许分批装运。

3. When is the earliest we can effect the shipment?

   最早什么时候可以装船？

4. Since there is no direct vessel, we have to arrange multimodal combined transport by rail and sea.

   由于没有直达船只，我们只好安排海陆联运。

◆ Insurance

1. As for the insurance arrangements, we'll leave them to you, but we wish to have the goods covered against Fresh Water Damage.

   保险事宜由你方安排，但希望该货物保淡水雨淋险。

2. May I ask what exactly insurance covers according to your usual CIF terms?

   请问根据你们常用的到岸价条件，所保的究竟包括哪些险别？

3. What risks should be covered?

   您看应该保哪些险？

4. As usual, the goods have been insured in W.A. terms. Premium will be added to the invoice amount together with freight charges.

   按通常习惯，货已保水渍险。保险费连同运费合并在发票上。

5. The goods are to be insured...

   这批货投保……

6. You must bear/ pay for the premium for this sort of special coverage.

   你们必须自己承担这类风险的保险费。

◆ Packing

1. How are you going to pack our goods?

   你打算怎样包装我们的货物？

2. I'm afraid your cartons are not strong enough to stand rough handling in transit.

   恐怕纸箱不够结实，经受不住这样重的货物，也经受不住运输中的野蛮搬运。

3. We request that you reinforce the packing with straps.

   我们要求用条带加固纸箱。

4. We can meet your special requirements for packing, but the extra expenses should be borne by you.

   我们可以满足你方包装的特殊要求，但额外的费用由你方承担。

Role-play

At the Canton Fair, after agreeing on the price, quantity and payment terms of the washing machines, Shillton Household Equipment Company and Haier Group move on to the discussion of the shipment of the goods. Haier Group proposes transshipment since liner space to Europe has been fully booked up while Shillton Household Equipment Company prefers direct shipment. Work in pairs and role-play the conversation. Swap roles and practice again. Some sentences are listed for your reference.

1. Can you make a prompt shipment?

2. How you are going to ship our goods?

3. What kind of insurance are you able to provide for my consignment?

4. Since there is no direct vessel, we have to arrange multimodal (多种方式的) combined transport by rail and sea(海陆联运).

5. I see your point, but ...

6. The last thing we want to do is to disappoint a customer, particularly an old customer like you.

Speak

Read the passage below and discuss the effective shipment negotiation strategies, then make a presentation on it.

Develop Your Negotiation Strategy for Better Shipping Terms

Shrewd (精明的) people in business know that the shipping industry can offer great savings opportunities. To identify these, you have to have a keen (敏锐的) eye. The following are some of the elements that help strengthen your negotiation strategy to obtain better shipping rates (运费).

Budget

You should have a price you are unwilling to go above according to your business model. Think about the question: What's the ideal and best price you are willing to offer for the shipping service?

BATNA

BATNA means Best Alternative to a Negotiated Agreement (最佳替代方案).It's a set of alternative (供选择的) options you can take if you cannot reach a viable (可行的) deal in your negotiation. A well-planned BATNA enables you to recognize a bad deal and gives you the courage and confidence to walk away.

Timelines

Time constraints (约束) can also be important to your negotiations strategy. The earlier you start negotiations with shipping companies, the less stressful you will be to conclude a deal, the more time you'll have to reach a mutually (互相地) beneficial agreement.

The Urgency of Delivery

Your strategy should state clearly how fast you need the products to be delivered. Compared with two or three days of delivery, same-day deliveries are often more expensive. The delivery time constraints rely on the nature of your goods and the promises that you make to your clients.

Payment Terms

Admittedly with one-off (一次性) payment, one can get attractive discounts; however, they can also be quite risky. It's safer to make payments in installments (分期) and keep the shipping company committed until the final payment. Well-balanced payment terms can not only guarantee that your shipping company delivers your products on time, but also limit your financial risk.

Concessions

Plan the concessions (让步) that you can give before the negotiation. Do some research, find concessions that can create value for the shipping company and present them in your meeting. The negotiation process can become very challenging if you are too rigid.

Use Third-Party Logistics Providers (3PL)

Third-Party Logistics Providers (3PL) (第三方物流) provide a useful service by shipping your cargo via their own intermodal (联运的) networks. A trusted 3PL provider can not only manage all the regulatory and intermodal networking issues you may face but also help you connect and share shipping costs with other dealers in your vicinity. It can save you both time and money and allow you to focus on your core business.

Negotiate with Other Shipping Companies

Before signing off on a deal, make sure you have exhausted your other options. Do not deal with only one shipping company, or you might miss a better option. In a comprehensive (综合的) negotiation seminar, you can learn how to leverage competitive bids to secure better deals.

Round-Up

The shipping industry presents smart people in business with a great number of opportunities to negotiate better deals. The techniques in this passage are not exhaustive (详尽的). However, they can set you on the right track and feed into your strategy.

Module 4　Signing a Contract

Watch

Task 1　Watch the video and decide whether the following statements are *True* (T) or *False* (F).

1. None of them suggests having another check of the contract before signing it.　　（　　）

2. The contract has been written in English only.　　（　　）

3. The goods will be shipped in containers.　　（　　）

4. Partial shipments are not allowed.　　（　　）

5. Andy and Baron finally make the deal successfully.　　（　　）

Task 2　Fill in the blanks with the missing words based on the video.

1. Yes, but we'd better have another check to avoid arguing over some _____ in the days to come.

2. Let's check all the items and make sure that no important items are _____.

3. Both languages are equally _____.

4. There are two of the _____ of the contract.

5. Almost _____ are clearly stated as we've discussed earlier.

6. Well, in that case, we can spend some time on them and see what we can do with them for our _____.

7. Sure. I really appreciate your _____!

8. Well then, all that's left is to _____.

9. Yes, I'm so pleased that we _____ finally.

10. I hope the contract will lead to years of _____.

Task 3　Watch the video again and choose the best answer to each question.

1. What languages was the contract written in?

    A. Chinese and French   B. English and French

    C. Chinese and Spanish   D. English and Chinese

2. What does Baron want Andy to do with the contract by giving him a copy of it?

    A. to revise it   B. to rewrite it

    C. to check it   D. to sign it directly

3. Why does Andy ask for a moment when he is given a copy of the contract?

    A. Because he needs it to read through the contract.

    B. Because he needs it to sign the contract.

    C. Because he needs it to contact his business partners.

    D. Because he needs it to contact his boss.

4. If Baron can't get all the products ready before the end of this month, what kind of shipment would be allowed?

A. Direct shipment   B. Partial shipment   C. Transshipment   D. Not mentioned

5. Can you infer from the conversation how Andy and Baron feel about the deal?

A. dreadful   B. surprised   C. pleased   D. playful

Task 4 **Work in pairs and summarize the key points of the conversation. Then, try to retell the story in the video.**

Learn

Learn the following *Words & Phrases* and *Sentence Drills*.

Words & Phrases

minor *adj.* 较小的

overlook *v.* 忽略

effective *adj.* 有效的

original *n.* 原件

clause *n.* 条款

sign *v.* 签名

cooperation *n.* 合作

mutual benefit 互惠互利

close the deal 完成交易

partial shipment 分批装运

in order 整齐，清晰

Sentence Drills

◆ **Checking the contract**

1. Shall we sign the contract now?
   我们现在可以签合同了吗？

2. Is there anything to be amended?

还有需要修改的地方吗？

3. We'd better have another check.
   我们最好再检查一下。

4. I'm afraid that there are still some clauses that might need further discussion.
   恐怕还有一些条款需要进一步讨论。

5. We'd like to have the words "..." in the contract.
   我们希望把这些话"……"写进合同中。

◆ **Expressing excitement about the deal**

1. I hope the contract will lead to years of pleasant cooperation.
   希望这个合同是今后多年愉快合作的开始。

2. Let's propose a toast to our cooperation!
   为我们的合作干杯！

3. I'm so pleased that we close the deal finally.
   我很高兴我们终于达成了交易。

4. Frankly, I've been looking forward to this moment for a long time.
   坦白说，我期待这一刻已经很久了。

Role-play

After several rounds of negotiations, Shillton Household Equipment Company and Haier Group finally reach an agreement and are going to sign the contract. When checking the contract, Shillton Household Equipment Company suggests that a minor modification be made to the shipping terms of the contract. They don't allow transshipment so they'd like to have "transshipment prohibited" stated clearly in the contract. Work in pairs and role-play the conversation. Swap roles and practice again. Some sentences are listed for your reference.

1. Shall we sign the contract now?

2. We'd better have another check.

3. I'm afraid that there are still some clauses that might need further discussion.

4. We'd like to have the words "transshipment prohibited" in the contract.

5. I hope the contract will lead to years of pleasant cooperation.

Speak

Read the passage below and discuss how to draw up a contract, then make a presentation on it.

Drawing Up a Contract for the Purchase

Once all the points such as price, delivery times, payment terms, etc. have been negotiated and a deal has been agreed to, it's time to draw up a written contract and get it signed by both parties (双方) . Although verbal (口头的) contracts are acceptable and legally binding (有约束力的) , they're very hard to rely on in court.

Both parties should reach an agreement on what the contract will cover. Typically, it will include the following: details of price, payment terms and delivery schedule, a clause stating the supplier's right to ownership (所有权) of the goods until they're fully paid for, and a clause limiting the seller's contractual liability (责任) — taking into consideration the purchaser's statutory (法定的) rights.

The terms and conditions used to depend on who holds the bargaining power in the negotiations. It can be the supplier's, the purchaser's, or a mixture of the two. One of the most important things is that one should get legal advice on drawing up the standard terms and conditions. The aim, of course, is to get a contract that protects one's own interests and that shifts legal responsibility for any problems to the other party.

It's a good idea to explicitly (明确地) ask about any requirements or any hidden problems and to keep a written record of all assurances given. Besides, write into the contract explicitly what will happen if there are any problems with the goods or services. For instance, will the supplier replace individual faulty goods (次品) or the whole batch (整批) and within what period? Any after-sale service? How to deal with the purchaser's failure to fulfill his duty? What are the penalties (处罚) for failure to meet delivery times or quality standards? Any future discount?

Last but not least, it's also important to include any dispute resolution (调解纠纷) or exit procedures that must be followed if either party is dissatisfied with the relationship or wants to end the contract.

Module 5   Further Exploration

Student A, a journalist for a program from Guangzhou TV—*Approaching International Trade*, is interviewing student B, a successful entrepreneur of SKY Furniture Trading Company about international trade.

❖ Student A tries to invent any details to finish the program.

❖ Student B tries to clearly explain exporting jargon (行话) or common trading terms and international trading customs based on the following passage.

❖ Use as many words and expressions in the following passage as possible.

Swap roles and practice again.

Common Terms Used in International Trade

1. Incoterms

Incoterms short for International Commercial Terms, are legal commercial terms used to determine who is responsible for what during the shipping process. Generally speaking, every Incoterm does one of two main things. One is to determine at what point the responsibility and ownership for the shipment transfers from the seller to the buyer. This is important in case the goods are lost or damaged in shipment. The other is to determine who takes responsibility for the transportation of the goods, import and export processes, insurance, loading and unloading, so on and so forth. Roughly speaking, there are three types of Incoterms.

• EXW, FCA, FAS and FOB. With these, the shipping costs are paid by the buyer, so it's advantageous for the exporter.

• CFR, CIF, CPT and CIP. With these terms, though the sellers pay for the main shipping costs, the buyer will want to investigate insurance since the goods travel at the buyer's risk.

• DAT, DAP and DDP. It's the seller that pays for the shipping costs and it's also the seller that assumes all the travel risk. So the seller will want to consider insurance.

2. Shipping terms

Logistics

As is known to all, it's complex to ship the goods. Fortunately, you don't have to do it alone. There are lots of partners, such as the International Freight Forwarders Association, that regulate the industry. Go to the CIFFA site to find out about the legitimate freight companies in your area.

Customs brokers

Similarly, the Canadian Society of Customs Brokers can help make shipping easier. It's an umbrella organization for those who can help you with customs (海关) issues.

Cargo insurance

Since carriers provide only minimal compensation, if a container falls overboard in rough seas or a package is lost at a cargo airport, it's better to get cargo insurance. There are clauses, known as Institute Cargo Clauses A, B, or C, that are internationally recognized and in this case, all companies have the same clauses, no matter what company you deal with. A covers all risks. B and C are cheaper, but they cover less.

The same applies to other modes of transport. In trucking in Canada, the maximum liability of a trucker is $2 per pound of freight or $4.41 per kilogram. In the U.S., it can be as low as 60 cents per pound.

As for shipping through air freight, the maximum liability depends on the nationality of the airline, but generally, they pay around $30−35 per kilogram.

Ocean freight varies, usually running from $500 to $900 per container. Thus, we can see that cargo insurance is even more important for ocean freight.

Wood packaging materials

If wood, such as pallets or crates (板条箱) , is used in shipment, you're bound by international regulations. The wood is supposed to be heat-treated or fumigated (烟熏消毒) and certified with a stamp when shipped to any place except the U.S. Failure to use treated wood would result in the rejection of the shipment at the other end. This only applies to non-manufactured wood, not to plywood (胶合板) and chipboard. Canada and the U.S. have a mutual exemption on this, but in case things change, it's a good idea to know these rules now.

Commercial invoice

On the invoice, what's included are the seller, buyer, origin of the goods and Incoterm to indicate who is paying for what. This is the most important document because it's what will be used at customs. It's recommended (推荐) , though not compulsory (强制的) , to also give a packing list.

Pro forma invoices

These are similar to the commercial invoice concerning the content, except they're for items going to another country but not being sold there – such as samples at a trade show.

3. Terms for payment options

As for this part, you can refer to *Module Two Negotiating about Payment* of this unit.

Module 6   Simulation Workshop

Step 1   Project Background

After listening attentively to the introduction of Ivy Xie from SKY Furniture Trading Company of their exhibits at the Canton Fair, George Parker from ABC company goes back to discuss with his boss Andy Hathaway and decides to place an order for tables and folding chairs. The next day, George Parker and his boss Andy Hathaway come back to the exhibition booth of SKY Furniture Trading Company at the Canton Fair and hold a negotiation with Ivy Xie and her sales manager Baron Li in terms of the price, quantity, payment and other terms, such as shipment, packing and insurance. After several rounds of negotiation, the two parties finally successfully sign the contract on the last day of the Canton Fair before they dismantle the booth.

Step 2   Suggested Preparations

1. Roles Assignment

Form a team with 4 students. Then, decide roles for each team member who undertakes the corresponding task, such as asking and negotiating about price, payment, shipment, packing and insurance.

2. Collect Information

Collect necessary information and get ready for presentation.

3. Rehearse and Make Improvements

Have a rehearsal about the presentation and make improvements if necessary.

Step 3   Shoot a Video

Shoot a video about the whole negotiation process. Hand in your video in a week and your teacher will rank and award the top 3 videos.

❖ **Self-assessment**

Assess according to the following table and find out what progress you have made.

Learning Assessment

Assessment Content	Assessment Standard	Total Score	Self-Assessment Result	Your Score
Listening Activity	I can get the right answer for the listening tasks.	10		
	I can grasp the general idea of the listening materials.	10		
	I can detect the details of the listening materials.	5		
	I can take notes when listening to classmates' presentations.	5		
Role-play and Speaking Activity	I can use the skills and conduct the tasks required in this unit.	5		
	I can talk about the subject and its relevant information in this unit.	5		
	I can play well in the role-play.	10		
	I can express and present my ideas about the subject and its relevant information.	10		
Reading Activity	I can understand the main idea of the text.	5		
	I can use the words, phrases and sentence patterns in the text to finish the speaking exercises.	5		
Pronunciation	I can pronounce the new words correctly with a standard tone and rhythm.	10		
Fluency and Coherence	I can use a range of connectives and discourse markers to express my ideas with logic and coherence.	10		
Grammatical Range and Accuracy	I can use a mix of simple and complex grammatical structures, but with limited flexibility.	10		
Total		100		

Post-show Work

Learning Objectives

❖ Familiarize with words and expressions on booth dismantlement, exhibition feedback and postexhibit report.

❖ Learn to dismantle display items and make follow-up contacts.

❖ Master the skills of listening and speaking concerning booth dismantlement, exhibition feedback and post-exhibit report.

❖ Develop the ability of communication, reflection, empathy and summary.

Warm-up

The goal of the exhibition is not only to exhibit but to increase the visibility of the company and its products, broaden the market, and expand the company's sales volume through the exhibition. Therefore, the end of the exhibition on-site does not mean that the work of this exhibition has been completed. To some extent, after-show work will determine the effectiveness of the company's exhibition. Besides the closing procedures of a trade fair, do remember to establish contacts, strengthen them and stay connected by following up soon after the closure of the trade fair event, as speediness shows your value on the clients and efficiency helps to improve the image of your company. In addition, exhibitors and visitors are supposed to give feedback on the services, organization and planning of the trade fair at the end of the exhibition to improve its effects in the future. After the fair, exhibitors are also supposed to make a post-show report by analyzing the results and offering improvement measures. In short, to provide timely follow-up service to the target clients according to their types and requirements of those visiting the exhibition and then adopt different follow-up methods to develop, consolidate and maintain the relationship with the clients is the focus of the follow-up work, which helps to achieve the corporate goals and ensures the results of the exhibition.

Discuss the following questions in pairs based on the background knowledge above.

1. What do exhibitors need to consider when an exhibition comes to the end?

2. What feedbacks would exhibitors give to the host?

3. What might an exhibitor report to the company after the show?

Module 1　Discussing Booth Dismantling

Watch

Task 1　Watch the video and decide whether the following statements are *True* (T) or *False* (F).

1. Ivy is responsible for arranging the tear-down of the booth.　　　　　（　）

2. Baron said that they can break down the wall panels.　　　　　　　　（　）

3. They do not need to move out their exhibits.　　　　　　　　　　　（　）

4. If they do not follow the dismantling instructions, they will be fined.　（　）

5. Not all accessories are recyclable.　　　　　　　　　　　　　　　　（　）

Task 2　Fill in the blanks with the missing words based on the video.

1. The exhibit will end in three days. Have you _____ the move-out?

2. According to the regulations and rules on dismantlement, here are some instructions we need to _____.

3. First of all, we are not allowed to _____, amend, destroy or deface the exiting building or all permanent facilities.

4. _____, the floor and walls as well as the wall panels of the booth may not be nailed or holed.

5. Ok, I will _____ it. What else?

6. I will _____ and keep you posted.

7. Thanks. And we must get _____ in advance.

8. Workers only with a _____ Pass for booth dismantlement may enter the exhibition halls.

9. I will make sure the team will be informed, so we won't _____ paying a penalty charge.

10. You are _____. Do you have any questions?

Task 3　Watch the video again and choose the best answer to each question.

1. When do they arrange the dismantlement?

　　A. before the exhibition　　　　　　B. during the exhibition

　　C. after the exhibition　　　　　　　D. on the last day of the exhibition

2. They might be allowed to _____ the exiting building?

　　A. amend　　　　B. destroy　　　　C. draw on　　　　D. clean

3. Why should the pushcarts have rubber or nylon wheels?

　　A. to be easily pushed　　　　　　　B. to protect the exhibits

　　C. to avoid scratching the floor　　　D. to be more beautiful

4. Which one is not mentioned by Baron that may not be nailed or holed?

　　A. the poster　　　B. the floor　　　C. the wall panels　　　D. the wall

5. How many rules do they need to follow?

   A. 3   B. 4   C. 5   D. 6

Task 4　Work in pairs and summarize the key points of the conversation. Then, try to retell the story in the video.

Learn

Learn the following *Words & Phrases* and *Sentence Drills*.

Words & Phrases

instructions *n.*　操作指南

dismantle *v.*　拆卸

amend *v.*　修改

deface *v.*　乱涂，乱写

permanent *adj.*　永久的

facility *n.*　设施

nail *v.*（用钉子）固定

valid *adj.*　有效的

inform *v.*　通知

penalty *n.*　处罚，惩罚

accessory *n.*　配件，配饰

landfill *n.*　垃圾填埋场

recyclable *adj.*　可回收利用的

deadline *n.*　最后期限

wall panel　墙板

release form　放行条

Sentence Drills

◆ **Coherence in a conversation**

1. First of all, we are not allowed to dismantle, amend, destroy or deface the exiting building all permanent facilities.

   首先，我们不能拆除、修改、破坏或者涂改现有的建筑物以及所有永久设施。

2. In addition, the floor and walls as well as the wall panels of the booth may not be nailed or holed.

   此外，地板、墙面以及展位的墙板不能钉钉子或者打孔。

3. For moving our furniture outside the exhibition halls, pushcarts with rubber or nylon wheels are requested.

   要搬展厅外的家具，必须用带橡胶或尼龙轮子的手推车运送。

4. Do remember that workers only with a valid Pass for booth dismantlement may enter the exhibition halls and must go through the security check.

   一定记住，在撤展期间佩戴有效通行证的工人才能进入展厅，而且必须过安检。

◆ **Answering in a conversation**

1. All right, I will take them down.

   好的，我会记下来的。

2. OK, I will keep an eye on it. What else?

   好的，我会注意的。还有其他需要注意的吗？

3. I will see to it and keep you posted.

   我会负责并随时向您汇报进展。

4. Got it! I will make sure the team will be informed, so we don't end up paying a penalty charge.

   明白！我会确保团队都了解这些操作，这样我们才不会被罚款。

Role-play

Work in pairs and deal with the exhibits (展品) after the show. Student A, a stand staffer, initiates a conversation with a packing worker, Student B.

❖ Student A tries to explain to Student B how to deal with the exhibits after the show.

❖ Student B tries to make sure different exhibits should be treated differently.

❖ Use as many words and expressions in the Sentence Drills as possible.

Swap roles and practice again. Some sentences are listed for your reference.

1. Should the chairs be packed and transferred to the next show?

2. The small items can be left as giveaways (赠品) since the transporting fee is too high.

3. We will abandon those that have been damaged.

4. How do you deal with the large furniture?

Speak

Read the following advice for stand staffers. Make a presentation on Tips for Dismantling.

Tips for Dismantling

Rules for booth dismantlement differ from country to country. Many countries do not have unionized labor and some may not even offer services that require skilled labor. Even if forklifts are available, local culture may require that more traditional methods be used such as manual labor to move and position exhibits. At the end of the trade show, it is not unusual to work through the night to break down a show and move it out. To avoid blocking the subsequent exhibit, here are some tips for booth dismantling.

◆ Communicate with the leader on the dismantling team ahead of time to discuss the details and your expectation. Exchange contact information in case something unexpected comes up so that all the parties involved know how to get a hold of each other.

◆ Be sure to arrange for the necessary tools and equipment.

◆ Print and email copies of line drawings, renderings (透视图) , and staging photos of your exhibit design.

◆ Make notes and take photos to help describe any little tricks, tips, or special attention details for dismantling any of the complicated components.

◆ Hold a brief meeting with the dismantling team right before the dismantlement. Make the team informed of all the dismantling instructions. Sketchy verbal directions left behind for service personnel are not enough.

◆ You have the right to request a change if you find that a member of the dismantling team performs poorly. Tell the leader of the team that you need someone more experienced.

◆ As units are dismantled, panels, parts, and display products must be checked for damage. A list of damaged or marred (损坏的) elements must be prepared. This is especially true for exhibits that move from show to show without exhibit house intervention.

◆ Exhibits are sent out with spare fittings, built-in boxes for bolts, basic setup materials such as tapes, wire, touch-up paint (润色漆), brushes, and even special tools.

◆ Make travel plans with the removal process in mind.

Module 2　Giving Feedback to the Host

Watch

Task 1　Watch the video and decide whether the following statements are *True* (T) or *False* (F).

1. It is the first time for Ivy to meet Jeffery Lee. 　　　　　　　　　　　　(　)

2. Ivy is satisfied with the fair. 　　　　　　　　　　　　　　　　　　　(　)

3. Ivy wants to see more foreign media but fewer audiences. 　　　　　　　　(　)

4. Sometimes the exhibition halls were too crowded. 　　　　　　　　　　　(　)

5. Ivy will participate in the fair again. 　　　　　　　　　　　　　　　　(　)

Task 2　Fill in the blanks with the missing words based on the video.

1. I wonder if you could _____ me a few minutes.

2. I would like to get_____ from you.

3. It is very _____. Our participation proved to be worthwhile and productive and we have attained many new contacts.

4. What about the _____ and planning of the fair?

5. No complaints. We _____ the arrangements.

6. That is _____. Could you give us some suggestions so that we could do a better job next time?

7. I think it would be better to have more _____.

8. With the _____, I believe we will attract more foreign media next year.

9. The number of audiences was _____ our expectation.

10. I am looking forward to _____ you in the next fair.

Task 3　Watch the video again and choose the best answer to each question.

1. What does Ivy think of the fair?

　A. She is satisfied.　　　　　　　　B. She has some complaints.

　C. She reckons it is not successful.　　D. She regrets she participated.

2. Why does Jeffery want to talk with Ivy?

　　A. to collect the questionnaire　　　　　B. to give Ivy a questionnaire

　　C. to thank Ivy for her hard work　　　　D. to ask for Ivy's feedback

3. What does Ivy think of the organization and planning of the fair?

　　A. She wants to complain.　　　　　　　B. She thinks it is satisfactory.

　　C. She wants to give some suggestions.　　D. She hates it.

4. Which of the following does Ivy complain about?

　　A. the traffic　　　B. the venue (场地)　　　C. the accommodation　　　D. the number of audiences

Task 4　Work in pairs and summarize the key points of the conversation. Then, try to retell the story in the video.

Learn

Learn the following *Words & Phrases* and *Sentence Drills*.

Words & Phrases

spare *v.*　留出，空出

questionnaire *n.*　调查问卷

worthwhile *adj.*　值得（花费时间、金钱或努力等）的

productive *adj.*　富有成效的

complaint *n.*　抱怨

encouraging *adj.*　令人振奋的

exposure *n.*　曝光

beyond *prep.*　超出

reserve *v.*　预订

corporate image　公司形象

Sentence Drills

◆ **Asking for opinions**

1. So what do you think of the fair?

　　请问您觉得展会如何呢？

2. What about the organization and planning of the fair?

　　请问您觉得展会的组织和安排如何呢？

3. Could you give us some suggestions so that we could do a better job next time?

　　请问您能否给我们一点意见以帮助我们把工作做得更好呢？

4. Is there any other thing we can improve?

　　请问还有什么是我们可以改进的吗？

◆ **Expressing satisfaction**

1. It is very successful.

　　我认为非常成功。

2. No complaints. We are satisfied with the arrangements.

　　没有可抱怨的。我们对所有的安排都感到满意。

3. That is encouraging.

　　那真让人振奋。

Role-play

Jeffery Smith, a staffer from the Fair Committee, is responsible for collecting feedback on the Fair from the exhibitors. Lee Wei is a stand staffer in HOMI MILANO supplying skin-care products. Jeffery is asking for opinions from Lee Wei by a questionnaire. Work in pairs and role-play the conversation. Some sentences are listed for your reference.

1. What do you think of the accommodation?

2. How do you like the service of the contractors?

3. Is the brand exposure satisfactory?

4. What is your complaint?

5. That's exactly what I think.

6. I couldn't agree with you more.

Speak

Read the passage below and discuss how to make a questionnaire. Then make a presentation on it.

How to make a questionnaire

Getting feedback from the exhibitors, visitors or other attendees is one of the post-show jobs for the host of an exhibition. The results can lead to decision-making and policy changes if the feedback is sound. Only if the questionnaire is designed properly, can the results be straightforward and reliable.

1. Decide what you want to know about from your questionnaire. Plan what data you need and how you will use it, which will help you come up with useful questions.

2. Design questions. Begin with a broad range of questions, and then narrow them down until each one relates to your goals in some way. Make sure the questions and answers are short and simple.

3. Use closed-end questions to gather specific answers. These questions include yes-or-no questions, true-or-false questions, or questions that ask the respondent to agree or disagree with a statement. They might look like these.

- Have you attended the Canton Fair before?
- How satisfied were you with your experience here? (The answers would be limited— "satisfied" or "dissatisfied")
- Would you recommend this fair to a friend?

4. Use open-ended questions to gather unanticipated information. These questions might look

like these.

- Who referred you to this fair?
- What kind of exhibition do you normally attend?
- What improvement can we make?

5. Ask straightforward and unbiased questions. Avoid using double negatives, unnecessary clauses, or unclear subject-object relationships.

6. Avoid grammatical and spelling mistakes. People will think it is a waste of time to fill in your questionnaire which is poorly presented or not grammatically correct.

7. Follow comfortably from the previous question. Group similar questions.

8. Do not imply a desired answer like: Wouldn't you like to receive our free brochure?

9. Do not use unfamiliar words or abbreviations.

10. Do not use emotionally loaded or vaguely defined words.

Module 3   Reporting an Exhibition

Watch

Task 1   Watch the video and decide whether the following statements are _True_ (T) or _False_ (F).

1. The total sales amounted to 5 million dollars.   (   )

2. The total sales of last year were 6 thousand dollars.   (   )

3. Nicholas is satisfied with the results of the fair.   (   )

4. The visitors did not like their new products.   (   )

5. Nicholas doesn't approve more budgets for the next fair.   (   )

Task 2   Fill in the blanks with the missing words based on the video.

1. Please come in and _____.

2. Mr. Court, would you please _____ me a few minutes?

3. The fair was a huge success and _____ beyond our expectations.

4. And the profit rate _____ 15 percent.

5. And that is why we _____ this year.

6. We did receive _____ from the visitors.

7. Well, is it possible to add more _____ for the fair?

8. Well, can you _____ a written report on the results of the fair by next Friday?

9. Then we may talk about the budget according to the results at the _____?

10. No problem. I will _____ it.

Task 3 Watch the video again and choose the best answer to each question.

1. What does Baron think of the fair?

   A. It's better than he thought.

   B. It's worse than he thought.

   C. It's as bad as he thought.

   D. It is as good as he thought.

2. The total sales of this year _____.

   A. was less than that of last year

   B. was more than that of last year

   C. was 5,600,000 dollars

   D. was 4,400,000 dollars

3. Which of the following descriptions of visitors is true?

   A. The number of international visitors outweighed that of domestic ones.

   B. The domestic visitors were not interested in their new products.

   C. The international visitors were interested in their new products in particular.

   D. None of the above is true.

4. What does Nicholas think of adding a catalogue?

   A. It is unnecessary.

   B. It needs to be discussed at the meeting.

   C. It is beyond his expectation.

   D. It is necessary.

5. What does Nicholas think of adding a budget?

   A. It is unnecessary.

   B. It needs to be discussed at the meeting.

   C. It is beyond his expectation.

   D. It is necessary.

Task 4 Work in pairs and summarize the key points of the conversation. Then, try to retell the story in the video.

Learn

Learn the following *Words & Phrases* and *Sentence Drills*.

Words & Phrases

dramatically *adv.*　显著地，剧烈地

get down to　开始认真处理

sum-up meeting　总结大会

follow up　跟进

total sales　销售总额

amount to　共计

profit rate　利润率

Sentence Drills

◆ **Starting a conversation**

1. Is now a good time to talk?
   请问现在可以聊一聊吗？

2. Do you have a minute to have a quick chat?
   请问你有时间和我聊一聊吗？

3. Would you please spare me a few minutes?
   请问你有空聊一聊吗？

◆ **Talking about budget**

1. You mean you need more budgets for the next exhibition?
   你的意思是下一次展览你需要更多预

算吗？

2. Can you produce a written report on the results of the fair by next Friday?
   你能在周五之前完成有关展会结果的一个
   书面报告吗？

◆ **Answering in a conversation**

1. No problem. I will get down to it.
   没问题。我会着手处理的。

2. That's not how I see it.
   在我看来不是那样。

3. The fair was a huge success and absolutely beyond our expectations.
   展览会获得巨大成功，完全超出我们的
   预期。

4. We did have very good brand exposures.
   我们做到了很好的品牌曝光。

5. By the way, don't forget to follow up the potential customers as well as the contracted customers.
   顺便提一下，别忘了跟进那些签了合同的
   客户以及还没签合同的潜在客户。

Role-play

Baron Li, a sales manager of SKY Furniture Trading Company, has just returned from the Canton Fair. He is making a brief phone report of the fair to the vice president of the company, Nicholas Court, and will set a time and location to discuss the details of the results of the fair.

Work in pairs and role-play the conversation. Some sentences are listed for your reference.

1. I hope I am not disturbing you.

2. I am sorry for calling you this late.

3. I am calling to organize a time to meet.

4. You did a great job at the trade fair.

5. Would you mind meeting me at 8 o'clock?

6. Shall we meet in your office tomorrow morning?

Speak

Read the passage below and discuss how to analyze exhibition results. Then, make a presentation on how to write a post-exhibit report by answering the questions listed in the passage. Some sentences are listed for your reference.

1. Generally speaking, it is a successful trade fair. We have signed 120 purchase orders worthy of 5 million dollars.

2. It attracts many industry professionals, and is getting acknowledged by more and more international peers.

3. We have reached our objectives in attending the trade fair, including making connections and making sales.

4. During the exhibition, there were a total of 20,000 visitors who were from home and abroad and international visitors occupied 20%.

5. The customer leads we gained at the fair will help us build a much wider customer base.

6. Our personalized product can meet the client's exact requirements.

7. The quality and variety of our products are very competitive.

8. The presentation and packaging of our products still need to be improved.

9. The response is very encouraging.

How to Analyze Exhibition Results

Exhibitors need to do exhibition results analysis because it is a way to add value to the exhibition investment. If you can answer the following 10 questions, you will have a clear clue in the post- exhibit analysis.

1. Did you meet your planned objectives?

2. How many products did you sell?

3. How many new connections did you make?

4. How are you going to follow up on the leads? By letter, phone call or a information pack(资料包/信息袋)?

5. Why did you have a good or poor response to what you are offering?

6. What could you have done better?

7. Did people just walk straight by?

8. Did you have eye-catching graphics and an attractive booth design?

9. How did your prices compare? Were they competitive ?

10. Did you have enough stock or did you sell out?

After answering the questions above, you can summarize the main features and report the results to your boss or supervisor. The report generally includes introduction, findings, conclusions and recommendations.

Module 4   Further Exploration

Role-play

Student A, a journalist for a program from Guangzhou TV—*Share Your Story in Canton Trade Fair*, is interviewing student B, an exhibitor from SKY Furniture Trading Company about how to measure the success of an exhibition.

❖ Student A tries to raise questions on the topic.

❖ Student B tries to share opinions based on the following passage with specific examples.

Swap roles and practice again.

How to Measure the Success of an Exhibition

Exhibitions, shows and fairs provide the best opportunity for you to meet more new contacts in a short period. How to make the best of them depends on how to maximize their potentials. Therefore, knowing the way to measure the success of an exhibition is of great importance.

1. Track your budget

Keep track of your budget and after the show is over, work out a figure that includes absolutely everything you spent.

2. Count contacts or leads

Count the contacts or leads gained at the show and you can establish your cost per contact by dividing the total cost by the total number of leads.

3. Count orders

Keep track of the revenue gained as a result of the show and you can calculate your return on investment or ROI (Return on Investment).

4. Calculate your ROI

You will need to put a price on your success by calculating the return on investment.

5. Create a base for measurement

Knowing how well you have done gives you a benchmark to work from and improve upon.

Measuring the success of a trade fair should include the followings.

(1) the costs incurred

(2) details of contracts and information obtained

(3) analysis of visitor records

(4) stand visitors profile comparison (with the intended target group, those who attended previous trade fairs and the organizer's visitors)

(5) analysis of the exhibitors'questionnaire provided by the organizers

(6) consideration of the economic climate in the particular field

(7) advertising and invitation drive

(8) assessment of the stand itself — size, location, design

(9) the competence and degree of preparation of the stand personnel

(10) the results of the stand personnel's final assessment

(11) analysis of the performance of competitors

(12) press response to the company's participation in the trade fair

Module 5　Simulation Workshop

Step 1　Project Background

Baron Li, the sales manager of SKY Furniture Trading Company, has just returned from the Canton Fair. He has drafted a written post-exhibit report and is presenting the results to the relevant personnel in the sum-up meeting. Other people in the meeting will raise some questions in concern and Baron will be responsible for answering the questions. On the other hand, Nicholas Court, the vice president of the company, will discuss with the finance director David Clement about the budget for the next exhibition according to the report.

Step 2　Suggested Preparations

1. Roles Assignment

Build a team with 5 students. Then, decide roles for each team member who undertakes the corresponding task, such as presenting a report, raising questions and interrupting a conversation.

2. Collect Information

Collect necessary information and get ready for presentation.

3. Rehearse and Make Improvements

Have a rehearsal about the presentation and make improvements if necessary.

Step 3   Video Shooting

Shoot a video about the sum-up meeting. Hand in your video and your teacher will rank and award the top 3 videos.

❖ **Self-assessment**

Assess according to the following table and find out what progress you have made.

Learning Assessment

Assessment Content	Assessment Standard	Total Score	Self-Assessment Result	Your Score
Listening Activity	I can get the right answer for the listening tasks.	10		
	I can grasp the general idea of the listening materials.	10		
	I can detect the details of the listening materials.	5		
	I can take notes when listening to classmates' presentations.	5		
Role-play and Speaking Activity	I can use the skills and conduct the tasks required in this unit.	5		
	I can talk about the subject and its relevant information in this unit.	5		
	I can play well in the role-play.	10		
	I can express and present my ideas about the subject and its relevant information.	10		
Reading Activity	I can understand the main idea of the text.	5		
	I can use the words, phrases and sentence patterns in the text to finish the speaking exercises.	5		
Pronunciation	I can pronounce the new words correctly with a standard tone and rhythm.	10		

Continued

Assessment Content	Assessment Standard	Total Score	Self-Assessment Result	Your Score
Fluency and Coherence	I can use a range of connectives and discourse markers to express my ideas with logic and coherence.	10		
Grammatical Range and Accuracy	I can use a mix of simple and complex grammatical structures, but with limited flexibility.	10		
Total		100		

Business Follow-up

Learning Objectives

❖ Familiarize with words and expressions on exhibition follow-up.

❖ Learn to talk about after-show marketing activities and exhibition follow-up skills approprately in English.

❖ Master the listening skills concerning exhibition follow-up.

❖ Develop basic communicative skills in follow-up calls.

Warm-up

For all exhibitors, the end of an exhibition is the very beginning of the following business activities. By attending exhibitions, manufacturers hope to increase their visibility in the field, explore their market home and abroad, and gain great opportunities to showcase their products and services. Nevertheless, the work which may be more decisive to the exhibition usually occurs after it. So what marketing activities to hold afterward, how to follow up clients with different degrees of interest at the exhibition, and what skills to take when calling or visiting clients after the show become the main tasks of exhibition follow-up.

Discuss the following questions in pairs based on the background knowledge above.

1. When do you think the exhibitors should begin their follow-up?

2. What can the exhibitors do with the information from the exhibition?

3. Why the follow-up business may be more decisive to the exhibition?

Module 1　Post-show Marketing Activities

Watch

Task 1　Watch the video and decide whether the following statements are *True* (T) or *False* (F).

1. The number of visitors and inquiring buyers was much bigger last year.　　　(　　)

2. Two buyers placed orders that afternoon. ( )

3. This is Serena's first time attending the Canton Fair. ( )

4. Buyers are usually ranked by the sellers. ( )

5. Serena thinks follow-up is so complicated that she doesn't want to do it. ( )

Task 2　Fill in the blanks with the missing words based on the video.

1. The Canton Fair ended _____ ago.

2. I've finished all the _____ to the visitors who left name cards during the Canton Fair.

3. Is it too soon for the _____ marketing activities?

4. As it goes, make _____ while the sun shines.

5. We're likely to lose our leads to other _____ if we don't take the initiative?

6. Recently, we also communicate more on _____.

7. We can't _____ them to place an order, right?

8. What to say or write depends on which level we _____ the buyers at.

9. In that way, they are more likely to be _____.

10. So do we usually express our _____ firstly?

Task 3　Watch the video again and choose the best answer to each question.

1. When will Ivy begin the after-show marketing activities?

    A. tomorrow   B. in three days

    C. in one week   D. after the fair

2. Why would it be late if they don't take actions soon?

    A. Because there would be no buyers then.

    B. Because everyone would be too tired then.

    C. Because they may lose their clients then.

    D. None of the above.

3. What is the common way to follow up?

    A. emails

    B. phone calls

    C. social networks

    D. all of the above

4. What could be expressed for the first step of follow-up?

    A. order placement

    B. thanks for coming to the booth

    C. offer of more discount

    D. not mentioned

5. Which statement is NOT true according to the dialogue?

A. The urgency of order placement and the purchasing power are important elements for buyers' ranking.

B. For the buyers at a lower level, we should pay more attention and follow up more quickly.

C. After expressing our thanks to the buyers, we should continue to follow up a second time after a short period.

D. The after-show marketing activities are not so simple which take skills and patience.

Task 4   Work in pairs and summarize the key points of the conversation. Then, try to retell the story in the video.

Learn

Learn the following *Words & Phrases* and *Sentence Drills*.

Words & Phrases

inquire *v.*   询盘

previous *adj.*   以前的

session *n.*   （展会的）一期

timing *n.*   时机

follow-up *n.*   （展后）跟进工作

decade *n.*   十年

grade *v.*   给……分等级

indispensable *adj.*   不可或缺的

after-show marketing activities   展后营销活动

to a great extent   在很大程度上

social networks   社交网络

Sentence Drills

◆ **Talking about the post-show marketing activities**

1. It would be too late to follow up if we wait till the end of the fair or even one week after the fair.

如果等到展会全部结束，甚至一周之后再开始跟进，就太迟了。

2. Generally, we grade them according to their urgency of order placement and purchasing power.

一般来说，我们可以根据买家的订单紧急程度和购买能力进行分级。

3. Only more timely follow-up and more attention will make the clients feel more valued.

只有更及时跟进和更多的关注才会让客户有被重视的感觉。

4. The higher a buyer's level, the faster the follow-up.

级别越高的买家跟进得越快。

Role-play

Lee Wei is a stand staffer in HOMI MILANO supplying skin-care products and Mr. Lambert is a representative from ABC Company offering professional marketing advice. Lee is asking Mr. Lambert for advice. Work in pairs and role-play the conversation. Swap roles and practice again. Some sentences are listed for your reference.

1. Could you give us some tips on the post-show marketing activities?

2. Why is that so? / How can we do that?

3. Immediate follow-up shows them they are valued.

4. The first thing to remember is to follow up with potential customers one or two days after they come to our booth.

5. If we wait more than one week, the visitor leads will have been won over by the competitors.

6. It is also essential to screen all the leads to see who is a serious prospect.

Speak

Read the following passage about the exhibition follow-up by email, discuss with your partners and make a presentation on how to follow up after the exhibition.

After the Trade Show – Keep the Rapport Going

After the busy, tiring but rewarding trade show, business doesn't stop. It's time for the awesome follow-up! Like phone calls and visits, emails are traditional and effective ways to follow up.

First of all, you need a short and sweet subject line. Instead of using ineffective words like "invite" "join", and "confirm", try to throw in the visitor's name. Research shows that personalizing your subject line can increase open rates by 50%. Don't forget to make it clear that it's a follow-up email, or your email could probably be submerged with cold emails.

Keep the body of the email short, sweet, and to the point as well. Your main goal is to spark their memory of what company you are from and what you discussed at the trade show and then get a response. If there is an informative resource personalized to any prospect, be sure to include it in the email. Statistics show that the more time you forward your materials, the higher rate they read them. But keep it in mind not to send too frequently, nor too long time. It's also suggested to give them a link to your website, which might encourage them to click around and learn more.

Finally, give them an easy and straightforward call-to-action (CTA). Your CTA could be scheduling a meeting, linking them to a product demo, or asking them to name their single biggest challenge.

Once is never enough. Don't forget to follow up more than once — you'll increase your chances of success.

(Source: How to Follow Up with Leads After a Trade Show.https://mailshake.com/blog/trade-show-follow-up-email/, 2021-07-21)

Module 2   Following up Contracted Clients

Watch

Task 1   Watch the video and decide whether the following statements are _True_ (T) or _False_ (F).

1. Ivy is calling to inform George about the shipment.   (   )

2. The number of orders of SKY Company at the Canton Fair this year is much larger.   (   )

3. The rests of the goods will be delayed by about two to three months.   (   )

4. The ABC Company will bear the cost for the second delivery.   (   )

5. George chooses the second solution proposed by Ivy.   (   )

Task 2   Fill in the blanks with the missing words based on the video.

1. Our _____ supplier can't supply continuously, which may lead to the shipment delay of part of the products.

2. You know, many _____ have already placed an order with my company.

3. Have you got any _____?

4. Firstly, I'm so sorry for _____ trouble to you.

5. I'm still worried that some of my dealers may _____.

6. Then the other one is _____ shipment.

7. As for the rest, we can only deliver _____ time.

8. The biggest _____ we can offer is 5%.

9. But the _____ of two to three months is too long.

10. That's the _____ we can go to.

Task 3   Watch the video again and choose the best answer to each question.

1. What is the result of the problem of raw material supply?

   A. The order cancellation.   B. The delay of the shipment.

   C. The change of the raw materials.   D. The change of the product.

2. What does Ivy promise George?

   A. To prioritize their production of the rest.   B. To deliver more products for free.

   C. To offer more discount for the whole order.   D. To deliver the whole order right away.

3. How long will the rest of the goods be delayed approximately?

    A. two months   B. two to three months   C. three to four months   D. five months

4. How much discount do they agree on at last?

    A. 3%   B. 5%   C. 7%   D. 10%

Task 4 **Work in pairs and summarize the key points of the conversation. Then, try to retell the story in the video.**

Learn

Learn the following *Words & Phrases* and *Sentence Drills*.

Words & Phrases

shipment *n.* 装船，装货

supplier *n.* 供应商

partial *adj.* 部分的

contract *n.* 合同

priority *n.* 优先

prioritize *v.* 将……优先

dealer *n.* 经销商

approximately *adv.* 大概

awkward *adj.* 尴尬的，辣手的

raw material 原材料

ahead of time 提前

skillful manufacture 制作精良

user-friendly design 人性化设计

Sentence Drills

◆ **Expressing the worries**

1. I'm still worried that some of my dealers may cancel their orders for not being able to get the goods on time.

   我仍担心有的经销商可能因为不能按时收货而取消订单。

2. In that case, I'm not sure how many of my dealers can wait until the second arrival of goods.

   在那种情况下，我不确定有多少经销商会等到第二批货。

3. If those dealers cancel the orders with me, I may cancel the order of the rest of the goods as well.

   如果那些经销商同我取消订单，我剩余的那部分订单可能也要取消了。

◆ **Trying to keep the client**

1. We promise to give priority to your production as soon as we get the raw materials.

   我们承诺一拿到原材料就优先为贵公司生产。

2. We believe that the skillful manufacture and user-friendly design of our products can make it worth waiting.

   相信我们产品精良的做工和人性化的设计是值得等待的。

3. We'll arrange the shipment for you the moment the production is completed.

   生产一完成就马上为您安排装运。

Role-play

Task 1   Lee Wei is a salesperson of HOMI MILANO supplying skincare products and Chris Cooper is a buyer who placed an order with his company at the Canton Fair. Half a month has passed since the fair ended, but Chris hasn't made the advance payment. Lee is going to make a phone call to urge Chris to make the advance payment. Work in pairs and role-play the conversation. Some sentences are listed for your reference.

1. Without your advance payment, your production will probably be delayed.

2. I'm afraid the orders of other buyers will be put on production before yours.

3. I'm afraid the shipment of your order wouldn't be finished on time.

Task 2   Role-play a conversation of negotiation about the shipment delay. Student A, as a salesperson from SKY Furniture Trading Company in China, is negotiating with B, a client from ABC Company in the USA.

❖ Student A tries to invent as many details as possible to explain the causes of the shipment delay to Student B.

❖ Student B tries to express the worries to get more favorable terms.

❖ Use as many words and expressions in the Sentence Drills as possible.

Switch roles and practice again. The following sentences are listed for your reference.

1. I feel terribly sorry to tell you the bad news that the shipment is to be delayed.

2. I learned from the forwarder company that it is due to the busy season and the unexpected strike of workers these days.

3. But it would seriously delay the delivery to my clients.

4. This shipment is on a prior sale basis. I would be in a rather passive situation if it can't arrive on time.

Speak

Read the following list of problems that may occur after signing the contract with the buyers at the exhibition. Can you come up with any solutions to these problems? Discuss with your partners, then make a presentation on how to solve one or two problems out of the list.

Problems which may occur after signing the contract

Signing a contract with a buyer at an exhibition is not to say that all is well, as more problems may arise afterwards.

◆ A contract is only a purchase intention. If the buyer later looks for other similar products, he or she may find someone else to place an order.

◆ Even if an order is placed, the advance payment or letter of credit may be delayed for some reason.

◆ After the start of production, the seller should also pay attention to the problems in the production process, such as raw material supply, drawing, production line, quality control, and so on.

◆ After the completion of production, make sure that there is no delay in shipment.

◆ Finally, don't forget the problem of balance payment.

Module 3　Following up Potential Clients

Watch

Task 1　Watch the video and decide whether the following statements are *True* (T) or *False* (F).

1. Mr. Smith didn't have much impression on the products of SKY Company at the fair.　(　)

2. The products of SKY Company are very popular all over the world.　(　)

3. Mr. Smith has already got the material of company introduction.　(　)

4. The council table is a new design for SKY Company this year.　(　)

5. Ivy will send more detailed materials by email to Mr. Smith after the phone call.　(　)

Task 2　Fill in the blanks with the missing words based on the video.

1. It was so nice to meet you at the Canton Fair last week, and we had a very _____ conversation.

2. The products of your company are very _____.

3. Thank you for your _____ of our company and products.

4. Our company has a history of nearly 40 years in _____ office furniture.

5. I've got the material of your company introduction and _____.

6. Would you mind if I ask you which _____ you are interested in?

7. That office chair is a _____ design this year.

8. The chair is _____ in design, and it's quite comfortable to sit in.

9. This chair is designed _____ to the kinesiology principle.

10. I'll _____ it to you later after this phone call.

Task 3　Watch the video again and choose the best answer to each question.

1. In which area are the products of SKY Company popular?

　A. Asia　　　　B. Asia and Europe　　　C. Australia　　　D. Europe and America

2. What products is Mr. Smith interested in?

　A. The file cabins and chairs.　　　　B. The chairs and tables.

　C. The tables and shelves.　　　　　D. The chairs and shelves.

3. Which design is developed this year?

    A. The file cabin with a safe.   B. The council table.

    C. The flamingo-shaped chair.   D. The shelf made of blackwood.

4. Why does Mr. Smith like that chair design very much?

    A. The chair is unique in design.

    B. The chair is designed conforming to the kinesiology principle.

    C. It's quite comfortable to sit in.

    D. All of the above.

Task 4　Work in pairs and summarize the key points of the conversation. Then, try to retell the story in the video.

Learn

Learn the following *Words & Phrases* and *Sentence Drills*.

Words & Phrases

impressive *adj.* 印象深刻的

recognition *n.*　认可

newly-developed *adj.*　新开发的

specifically *adv.*　专门地

forward *v.*　推送，发送

product catalog　产品目录

council board　会议桌

have a good taste　有眼光，有品位

conform to　符合

kinesiology principle　人体工学

Sentence Drills

◆**Starting and developing a conversation of exhibition follow-up**

1. It was so nice to meet you at the Canton Fair last week, and we had a very pleasant conversation.

    很高兴在上周的广交会上认识您，并进行了一次愉快的交谈。

2. Thank you for your recognition of our company and products.

    感谢您对我公司和产品的认可。

3. Would you mind if I ask you which design you are interested in?

    介意问一下您对那款产品比较有兴趣呢？

4. I'll forward it to you later after this phone call.

    电话结束后我可以发送给您。

5. Please give me your feedback if you have any ideas.

    如果您有任何想法，也请反馈给我们。

◆**Expressing properly in the follow-up conversation**

1. The products of your company are very impressive.

    我对贵公司的产品有非常深刻的印象。

2. I've got the material of your company introduction and product catalogue at the fair.

    我在展会上已经拿到贵公司的介绍资料和产品目录。

3. And please forward me the one introducing the council board as well if there is.

    如果有类似的会议桌宣传册，也请发一份给我。

Role-play

Lee Wei is a salesperson of HOMI MILANO supplying skincare products, and Jessica White is a buyer who showed somewhat interest in the products of this company at the Canton Fair. Lee is going to make a phone call to follow up, trying to keep this client. Work in pairs and role-play the conversation. Some sentences are listed for your reference.

1. How was your journey to Guangzhou?

2. We have met at the trade fair. Do you have an impression of me?

3. It's not necessary to worry about the capability of our machining.

4. We'd like to order some customized products.

5. Our production period can be modified.

5. I'll inform you at once if there is any information about the new product.

Speak

Read the passage below about how to improve the follow-up calls. Then discuss with your partners about how you understand these 8 tips or come up with some examples for each tip.

Improve Your Follow-up Calls with These 8 Tips
By Erin Myers

In business, the follow-up is a fact of life. Now that texting has been more common than calling for a while, phone conversations aren't getting easier for many people. However, phone calls (and lately, video chats) are an important part of business communication — especially when you can't meet in person. When a customer reaches out to you, the way you handle that follow-up call can make or break your relationship with that customer. Here are some tried-and-true techniques to improve your follow-up calls and have more effective phone conversations.

1. Schedule your calls.

People are busy these days, and the chances of you catching them at an opportune time without making an appointment are slim. Scheduling your follow-up call is a polite and professional thing to do.

2. Be prepared.

People know when you're unprepared, and it's not a confidence booster. Instead of wasting their time and yours, do some prep work beforehand.

3. Ask questions that get answers.

This isn't as simple as avoiding "yes" or "no" questions. For many of us, asking effective questions aren't always easy. The questions you ask, as well as the questions you don't, have a major impact on the success of your conversations.

If you want to improve your follow-up phone conversations, you have to learn to ask direct, deliberate questions that result in useful answers. And you have to be comfortable remaining silent while the client responds.

4. Keep the conversation balanced.

A useful phone conversation requires equal parts of give and take. If you're doing all of the talking, you won't get the customer's input. But if you're doing all of the listening, then you're not asking the questions necessary to draw insight from the customer.

5. Ask follow-up questions.

Ask your questions and listen to the answers. Don't interrupt, but don't be afraid to ask follow-up questions if you need more information. Follow-up questions can also be useful in guiding the conversation, especially if you're talking to someone who is chatty or has trouble staying on topic.

6. Clarify answers by repeating them back to the client in your own words.

When you place an order at the drive-thru window, they often read the order back to you before ringing it up. This is done to ensure your order is correct. This same technique can work wonders when following up with clients.

7. Know how to use your phone.

This should go without saying, but how many times have you been on a call with someone who didn't know how to mute the phone, much less patch in an associate or transfer a call? If you're in a business where phone technology can make your follow-up calls complicated, make sure you know what you're doing before getting the client on the line.

8. Send a follow-up email to recap the call.

That's right — you should follow up the follow-up! After the call, compile the highlights of the conversation and any outstanding items that need following up. The purpose of this recap email isn't to provide a word-for-word summary of the conversation but to instead thank the client and recap the major talking points of the call for future reference.

(Source: Improve Your Follow-up Calls With These 8 Tips. https://www.outboundengine.com/blog/improve-your-follow-up-calls/,2021-7-21)

Module 4　Further Exploration

Role-play

The Canton Fair is going to end. Baron Li (Student A), a sales manager of SKY Furniture Trading Company is sharing with his team members Ivy Xie (Student B), salesgirl, and Serena Wang (Student C), a receptionist, about how to deal with different types of buyers during the follow-up period.

❖ Student B&C try to ask as many questions as possible.

❖ Student A tries to share experience based on the following passage.

❖ Use as many words and expressions in the passage below as possible.

Swap roles and practice again.

How to Follow up Different Types of Buyers

The period after the exhibition is the busiest time for us as foreign traders, for we have to immediately deal with the work delayed because of the exhibition, and at the same time, we have to follow up the buyers at the exhibition before they forget us and get good communication with them. At such a busy pace, is there any way to help us achieve the best effect of client development? Yes, categorize the clients.

At the exhibition, we can contact a large number of buyers, and the number of business cards we collect is also considerable. The first thing we do after the exhibition is to categorize these buyers so that we can better follow up and develop business relationships accordingly.

◆ **Buyers placing orders at the exhibition site**

This type of buyers will be the top priority for us to follow up because they have a strong sense of identity with us. At least for them, we are one of their supplier alternatives. We should keep in touch with and follow up such buyers in the exhibition, in a timely manner send the cooperation documents to them for confirmation, and remind them to make the advance payment.

Only the buyer who has made the advance payment is the real customer, and anything can happen before the advance payment is made. Even if a contract is signed, if a better supplier is found elsewhere, the order may be cancelled.

For buyers who place orders on-site, the operational space for us in the follow-up period is actually quite limited. Generally, the customers who can place orders at the exhibition are those with whom we have communicated deeply and negotiated simply. In many aspects, the negotiation has become an established fact and there is not much room for change. For such buyers, we have to carefully maintain the relationship with each other. Remember the point: be careful!

It is self-evident that such customers are important to us, but we do not have a high binding force on them. Therefore, we must be careful to deal with various problems and communicate with them carefully.

◆ Potential buyers with a deep impression

After all, there are very few buyers who can place an order on the spot, and some others are likely to stop by your booth and have a good conversation with you. Those who will talk to you in great detail, and show a strong interest in your products, everything from features to price terms to market prospects, belong to the group with high intention to purchase. This type of buyers is also the one we're most likely to approach.

Therefore, after the exhibition, we need to reply to their questions and send the materials they asked for during the exhibition for the first time, and carefully communicate with them. Generally speaking, this type of buyer who has talked to you in detail but hasn't placed orders must have doubts in some way. For example, they may have the requirement of having samples or visiting the factory first before order placement.

Even after following up on these problems, they still do not place the order; we should not be discouraged or even give up. Now that they have shown enough interest in us, there are still great opportunities for us to cooperate later, at least better than unfamiliar potential customers. So we still need to follow up every three to five weeks, such as sending an email, holiday greetings, and small gifts, etc.

◆ Buyers exchanging business cards after a simple contact

If the first two types are relatively smaller buyer groups in terms of quantity, then this third type of buyers who simply exchange business cards is the biggest harvest we have gained in the exhibition. This type of buyer is one of our important potential customer market resources, whose biggest characteristic is that they talk a few words with us, and have certain but not strong interests so they're often seen as alternatives.

For this type, we send them emails to express our thanks right after the exhibition. Then during the continuous follow-up, send the product information as detailed as possible according to their requirements, and express the hope for future cooperation.

Module 5   Simulation Workshop

Step 1   Project Background

Because of Ivy's excellent performance at the trade shows for the past five years, she is appointed to be responsible for the whole fair booth team the next year. The next Canton Fair is to open in one month. Ivy and her assistant Serena are going to have a short training for their booth team about all the business before, during, and after the exhibition.

Step 2   Suggested Preparations

1. Roles Assignment

Form a team with 5 students. Then, decide roles for each team member who undertakes the corresponding task, such as asking and answering questions, and trial demonstrations.

2. Collect Information

Collect necessary information and get ready for presentation.

3. Rehearse and Make Improvements

Have a rehearsal about the presentation and make improvements if necessary.

Step 3   Video Shooting

Shoot a video about the whole training of attending a trade fair. Hand in your video in a week and your teacher will rank and award top 3 videos.

❖ **Self-assessment**

Assess according to the following table and find out what progress you have made.

Learning Assessment

Assessment Content	Assessment Standard	Total Score	Self-Assessment Result	Your Score
Listening Activity	I can get the right answer for the listening tasks.	10		
	I can grasp the general idea of the listening materials.	10		
	I can detect the details of the listening materials.	5		
	I can take notes when listening to classmates' presentations.	5		

Continued

Assessment Content	Assessment Standard	Total Score	Self-Assessment Result	Your Score
Role-play and Speaking Activity	I can use the skills and conduct the tasks required in this unit.	5		
	I can talk about the subject and its relevant information in this unit.	5		
	I can play well in the role-play.	10		
	I can express and present my ideas about the subject and its relevant information.	10		
Reading Activity	I can understand the main idea of the text.	5		
	I can use the words, phrases and sentence patterns in the text to finish the speaking exercises.	5		
Pronunciation	I can pronounce the new words correctly with a standard tone and rhythm.	10		
Fluency and Coherence	I can use a range of connectives and discourse markers to express my ideas with logic and coherence.	10		
Grammatical Range and Accuracy	I can use a mix of simple and complex grammatical structures, but with limited flexibility.	10		
Total		100		

Scripts for Videos

(Background) Ivy Xie, the new salesgirl, and Baron Li, the sales manager, are both from SKY Furniture Trading Company. At the office, they are talking about exhibitions, because they are planning to participate in the upcoming China Import and Export Fair.

(Scene) At the sales manager's office of SKY Furniture Trading Company.

Baron: Good morning, Ivy. How's everything going?

Ivy: I'm fine, thanks. Just try to get adjusted. It's hard to keep track of everything around here.

Baron: As a newcomer, you need to learn a lot. You know we are planning to participate in the upcoming China Import and Export Fair.

Ivy: Yes, right now I'm learning something about exhibitions. But I am a little confused. Could I ask you some questions concerning exhibitions?

Baron: Sure, go ahead.

Ivy: What are the benefits of attending an exhibition?

Baron: That's a good question. We benefit a lot from attending an exhibition, for example, introducing our new products, publicizing our achievements or improving international influence. In short, the exhibition is one of the most effective media for establishing and maintaining customer relations.

Ivy: That's good. Another question: there are some similar terms like a trade show, fair, exhibition and expo, could you tell me their differences?

Baron: Sure. A trade show, as the name implies, is an event where companies in a specific industry gather to showcase and demonstrate their new products and services. Trade shows are B2B type of events. They are not open to the public.

Ivy: Then what is a fair?

Baron: A fair is a gathering of people for a variety of entertainment or commercial activities. There are different types of fairs, such as fun fairs for children, club fairs for students, temple fairs for the general public and trade fairs for buyers and sellers.

Ivy: How about an exhibition?

Baron: An exhibition has the least sales elements in it, the primary objective is to showcase products and services. Usually, an exhibitions covers one industry at a time and aims at building a general image of the company.

Ivy: What do you know about an expo?

Baron: An expo, or an exposition, is somewhere in the middle between a trade show and an exhibition. Expositions are open to the public, but focus very much on business networking as well, especially export opportunities. They are very large-scale events, usually international covering many industries, and may have government support. It's common for a lot of government organizations to play the role of exhibitors, for example, the Shanghai Expo.

Ivy: I'm still quite confused about all these terms.

Baron: Yes, you know, some people or countries prefer one term to the other. The term "Trade Show" is very popular in the US, whereas "Trade Fair" is traditionally more a UK term.

Ivy: Talking about the upcoming China Import and Export Fair, is it a trade fair or an expo?

Baron: Of course, it is a trade fair. It is also called the "Canton Fair" because it is regularly held every April and October in Guangzhou (or Canton). It is China's largest trade fair with the highest level, the most complete varieties, and the largest attendance and business turnover.

Ivy: Wow, that's very impressive. We should make every effort to prepare for it.

Baron: That's right.

Ivy: Thank you, Baron. Your suggestions are really valuable for me.

Baron: You can count on me. Feel free to turn to me for help if you meet any problems in your work.

Unit 1   Module 2

(Background) Ivy Xie, the new salesgirl, and Baron Li, the sales manager, are both from SKY Furniture

Trading Company. At the office, they are talking about different types of exhibitions, because they are preparing for the upcoming China Import and Export Fair.

(Scene) At the sales manager's office of SKY Furniture Trading Company.

Baron: Good morning, Ivy. You know we are going to attend the upcoming China Import and Export Fair. How much have you learned about exhibitions?

Ivy: Good morning. Thanks to my dear colleagues' help, I've already had some primary knowledge about exhibitions, but I am still puzzled about the different types of exhibitions. How can we classify exhibitions?

Baron: Well, exhibitions can be broadly categorized into three groups: art exhibitions, interpretive exhibitions, and commercial exhibitions.

Ivy: Could you please elaborate on that?

Baron: Sure. Art exhibitions, of course, display arts – sculptures, paintings, drawings, crafts, etc. Exhibits may belong to one artist, one group or one theme.

Ivy: What are interpretive exhibitions?

Baron: Interpretive exhibitions involve more text and graphics than art exhibitions. Exhibitions related to historical and scientific themes belong to this category.

Ivy: As for the commercial exhibitions, the Canton Fair must belong to them, am I right?

Baron: Yes, you are right, but commercial exhibitions can also be categorized into three major groups: B2B exhibitions, B2C exhibitions, and exhibitions that cater to both industries and consumers.

Ivy: What are the differences among them?

Baron: B2B exhibitions are often referred to as trade shows, and they bring together sellers and buyers of products and services in particular industrial sectors and are not open to the public while B2C exhibitions are often referred to as consumer shows, and they are open to the public. At consumer shows, companies gather not only to showcase their products and services but also to sell and market them.

Ivy: How about the exhibitions that cater to both industries and consumers?

Baron: Such exhibitions exhibit all types of consumer and industrial goods. They are open to the general public, but admit the public on certain days only.

Ivy: I get a better understanding of the exhibition industry now. Thanks a lot.

Baron: You're welcome.

Unit 1 Module 3

(Background) Ivy Xie, the new salesgirl, and Baron Li, the sales manager, are both from SKY Furniture Trading Company. At the office, they are talking about how to choose the right exhibition to attend.

(Scene) At the sales manager's office of SKY Furniture Trading Company.

Ivy: Good morning, Mr. Li.

Baron: Good morning, Ivy.

Ivy: I come here again to seek advice from you on how to choose the right exhibition to attend. I know many people make mistakes when choosing exhibitions.

Baron: You're right. Many exhibitors make mistakes of being loyal to their favourite shows even if they're not bringing back any results. And many choose the biggest and most popular event and simply hope to get a good return on investment.

Ivy: But how to avoid these mistakes and select the right exhibition?

Baron: First of all, you need to clearly define your objectives and figure out what you want to accomplish at the trade show. Do you want to increase leads and strengthen relationships with customers or just launch a new product or service and raise awareness about your company?

Ivy: Yes, I know. Only after we've clearly defined our objectives should we begin to search for trade show options.

Baron: You're right. When researching a trade show, you need to gather information on the industry and local market, identify your buyer's needs, and estimate how good a fit your product will be for the trade show's audience.

Ivy: Then what else should we focus on?

Baron: History. Once you've identified a list of potential trade shows, narrow down the list by taking a look at their history and past attendance. You need to know how much buying power the trade show has and how well the trade show does in terms of sales and networking.

Ivy: How about the location?

Baron: Yes, it's also a very important factor you should take into consideration. Usually, 40%–60% of attendees come from a 200-mile radius of the show location. Consider your distribution area and target audience.

Ivy: Is that all for the things we should consider when choosing an exhibition?

Baron: No. Last but not least is the budget. You should carefully plan the exhibiting budget and factor in all costs for each exhibition, not just the registration fees, space and your exhibition display, but also travel, hotel and on-site expenses, giveaways, marketing and promotions.

Ivy: Yes, if we are on a tight budget, we can do nothing but stay at home. Thanks a lot.

Baron: My pleasune.

Unit 2   Module 1

(Background) David, the General Manager of Canton Fair Advertising Co. Ltd., is discussing planning for organizing the 128th Canton Fair with Kathy.

(Scene) At the Canton Fair Advertising Co. Ltd.

David: Good morning, Kathy! I'd like you and Rachel to be involved in a big project.

Kathy: Morning, David. What's that?

David: We need to work out an exhibition proposal for the autumn session of the Canton Fair this year to get the ball rolling as quickly as possible.

Kathy: Great! This is the first time for me to organize such a big trade Fair. Could you please give me some suggestions?

David: You have already gained a lot of experience in organizing other exhibitions. I don't think it is a difficult task for you. I think building a team of about 10 members with the necessary skills and experience is the first thing you should do.

Kathy: Yes! Since the scale of the Canton Fair is huge, we need to set up a good team with those people who can work responsibly and also think independently.

David: Great! Now let's talk about some details that we should put into our exhibition proposal. We don't have to spend much time writing the "Exhibition Introduction" part. We can find out all the materials from the last session and do a little modification.

Kathy: What about "The Application" part?

David: Just as we did it before, asking the exhibitors to apply for admission to the Canton Fair online. As for the detailed application procedure, try to simplify the steps and make some improvements. As you know, making the process more convenient is one of our service goals.

Kathy: OK. Anything else?

David: Comfortable and convenient traffics and accommodations for exhibitors and visitors are important as well.

Kathy: I agree with you!

David: One more thing, the exhibition fees. They should vary for different exhibitors, for example, we should offer a discount for regular exhibitors and VIP exhibitors. And the fees for different types of booths (such as Island type, Peninsula type, End-cap type, Linear type, Corner type) should also vary from one to another, and please make sure they are reasonable.

Kathy: OK. I have already written this down in my notebook.

David: The last but not the least thing is the budget.

Kathy: Yes, we should make every penny count.

David: The budget is mainly used in publicity expenses and personnel costs. Alice and her marketing team will be in charge of exhibition publicity.

Kathy: OK. I will discuss this with Alice before making the budget. And we will be in full control of the budget.

David: Ok, I got it. One more thing, comfortable and convenient hotels and...

Kathy: When should I give you the exhibition proposal?

David: As early as possible. If things are arranged early in the planning process, we can avoid any last-minute problems.

Kathy: OK. I will give it to you by the end of this week.

David: Thank you!

Unit 2   Module 2

(Background) Kathy is in charge of the organization of the 128th Canton Fair, she is distributing assignments of publicizing exhibitions to her colleague Rachel.

(Scene) At Kathy's office.

Kathy: Rachel, please take your notebook and come to my office.

Rachel: OK. Anything I can do?

Kathy: A very important assignment.

Rachel: That's great. I'm ready to take up everything you give to me.

Kathy: There is only one month left before the opening of the 128th Canton Fair. It is time to publicize it now. I hope you can take charge of the publicizing job this time.

Rachel: OK. But I have little experience in publicizing exhibitions. Can you give me some guidance?

Kathy: Firstly, set up a website for the exhibition so that exhibitors and visitors can register and get tickets online. Do remember to link our website with several websites which are well-known in relevant industries. Then, make a list of our regular exhibitors and send them the invitations via E-mail.

Rachel: Do we need to telephone them?

Kathy: Of course! That's the second step. After sending them the invitations, we will call them to confirm whether they have received our invitation.

Rachel: I think it is proper to call them at least three days after sending the invitations, right?

Kathy: That's right!

Rachel: Apart from the regular exhibitors, new exhibitors are also very important. There are always some new companies who need our assistance to promote their products.

Kathy: I agree with you.

Rachel: But how can we develop new exhibitors effectively?

Kathy: Running ads in the newspaper, on TV as well as the internet, and some other mainstream media, like we do every year. But it is not very effective now. What's more, it is very costly.

Rachel: How about showing some publicizing videos on some online platforms? Such as Google, Baidu, Sina, Netease, Wechat, etc.

Kathy: That sounds great! We can have a try. We can also ask for assistance from the Ministry of Commerce of P. R. C. and the People's Government of Guangdong Province to share the link of the publicizing videos.

Rachel: What else should we do for new exhibitors?

Kathy: Since they are inexperienced, once we get in touch with them, we must provide them with enough materials. For example, some of them may have no idea about the design of the booths. We can recommend some reliable exhibition designing companies to them.

Rachel: OK. I will make a list of the exhibition designing companies.

Kathy: The new exhibitors should be contacted more times. So that we can know more about them and help them with their problems.

Rachel: Alright, one team is responsible for the regular exhibitors, another team responsible for the new ones.

Kathy: You hit the point. You are the right person to take up this task.

Rachel: Thank you!

Unit 2   Module 3

(Background) Rachel, an assistant from Canton Fair Advertising Co. Ltd., is calling George Parker from ABC company to invite him to attend the 128th Canton Fair.

(Scene) At Rachel's office.

Rachel: Hello! This is Rachel from Canton Fair Advertising Co. Ltd. Can I speak to George Parker?

George: Speaking, please.

Rachel: I am calling to invite you to the 128th Canton Fair. Have you received our invitation letter by email?

George: Yes, I have received your invitation letter. And I am planning to attend the 128th Canton Fair, but I'd like to know more about it. Would you like to tell me more about it?

Rachel: Well, the China Import and Export Fair, also known as the Canton Fair, is inaugurated in the spring of 1957, co-hosted by the Ministry of Commerce of P.R.C. and the People's Government of Guangdong Province and organized by the China Foreign Trade Centre.It is held every spring and autumn in Guangzhou, China. The Canton Fair is a comprehensive international trading event with the longest history, the largest scale, the most complete exhibit variety, the largest buyer attendance, the broadest distribution of buyer's source country, and the greatest business turnover in China.

George: Wow, impressive!

Rachel: Various types of business activities such as economic and technical cooperation and exchanges, commodity inspection, insurance, transportation, advertising, consultation, etc. are carried out in flexible ways. More and more business people at home and abroad are gathering in Guangzhou, exchanging business information and developing business friendships.

George: That sounds good.

Rachel: The Canton Fair is held two sessions a year, three phases each session. The spring session normally lasts from April 15th to May 5th and the autumn session from October 15 to November 5.

George: Yes. Maybe this year I can attend the autumn session. So how long does each phase last?

Rachel: There are 5 days for each phase and 3 days' break between the two phases.

George: Thank you. And how many stands were there at the Fair?

Rachel: During 126th Session there were 60,676 booths and the exhibition area of one session totalled 1,185,000 square meters.

George: May I know how many exhibitors and visitors attended it?

Rachel: In each session, there were 25,642 exhibitors including 25,000 exporters and 642 importers and about 200,000 buyers attended the Fair from more than 210 countries and regions all over the world.

George: So how about its export volume?

Rachel: The export volume amounted to CNY 207 billion (USD 29 billion) and the total number of overseas buyers reached 186,015. Actually, there were a great number of contracts and orders made after the fair.

George: That's a big sum of the transaction. I do think it's a great opportunity for me to attend this kind of fair.

Rachel: You are honorably welcomed. For further information, you can come to the official website: www.cantonfair.org.cn/en. If you plan to attend it, remember to download and fill in the application form and send it back to us at least 10 days in advance.

George: Where shall I send the application form?

Rachel: To the email address that is written at the bottom of the application form.

George: One more question, how much should I pay?

Rachel: It's free for you as one of our VIP clients.

George: Great! Please register our firm for a standard stand.

Rachel: OK. I will send you the registration form. Do remember to send back the forms before the registration deadline.

George: Sure! thank you so much!

Rachel: My pleasure. We are looking forward to seeing you at the fair.

George: Bye!

Rachel: Bye!

Unit 3   Module 1

(Background) George Parker and Bill Pullman, as visitors from ABC company, are going to attend the China Import and Export Fair (also known as the Canton Fair). They are queuing up for the security check at the entrance of the exhibition. Bill Pullman is the manager of the company.

(Scene) At the entrance of the Canton Fair.

George Parker: With so many people queuing up here, we need to wait a little longer.

Bill Pullman: Yes, there is always a sea of faces at the Canton Fair and we should wait patiently.

George Parker: This is my first time attending the Canton Fair. I am so excited.

Bill Pullman: This will be a rewarding trip for you.

George Parker: Is the security inspection strict at the entrance of the Canton Fair?

Bill Pullman: It's very strict. The Canton Fair implements a strict ID card inspection system. Passports used abroad must be inspected by relevant international institutions and verified again by domestic police.

George Parker: Do we just need to go through one entrance?

Bill Pullman: No, we need to go through three security checks. The first is a manual initial examination, the second is through the security door, and the third is card swiping and facial testing.

George Parker: It's so strict.

Bill Pullman: After entering the venue, you will find thousands of security personnel patrolling the venue at any time. Have you brought your exhibition certificates?

George Parker: ID card, exhibitor card and exit card are all here.

Bill Pullman: Is everything ready?

George Parker: Yes. Our company's information, computer, digital camera, business card, customer information registration form, small gifts, etc. are ready.

Bill Pullman: Good. Did the samples arrive yesterday? We must determine the time when the samples finally enter the venue and withdraw from the exhibition.

George Parker: Our samples arrived and we have made sure of the time. ... Bill, it's your turn. Move on.

(Bill goes ahead and takes the first security check)

Unit 3　Module 2

(Background) Ivy Xie, a salesgirl and an exhibitor from SKY Furniture Trading Company received the confirmation from the China International Furniture Fair. She is talking about building a booth with Baron Li who is the sales manager of SKY Furniture Trading Company, and then, calls Christina David who is the Sales Manager of the China International Furniture Fair to make sure the details.

(Scene) At Ivy's office.

Baron Li: What are you reading, Ivy?

Ivy Xie: They received our entry form and accepted us. We get an ideal booth in the middle of the first row. This is the confirmation.

Baron Li: That's great. Pay our entry fee in time.

Ivy Xie: Okay. The exhibition is in three weeks. We'll have much to do.

Baron Li: That's it. Call them and enquire about raw space installation.

(Ivy Xie called Christina David to enquire about raw space installation.)

Ivy Xie: Hello. This is Ivy Xie calling from SKY Furniture Trading Company. May I speak to Chris Davis?

Christina: This is Chris speaking. Hello, Ivy.

Ivy Xie: Hello, Chris. I'm calling to confirm with you about the raw space design and installation of the booth.

Christina: With pleasure. Please go ahead.

Ivy Xie: You recommended your official booth contractor X company to exhibitors. Do we have to use this company to design and build our company's booth?

Christina: Of course not. We select X company as our official booth contractor with strict standards. They have rich experience in providing booth designing installation services. You can choose other contractors if you have better options.

Ivy Xie: Thanks. We will think about it. What should we do if we choose other companies?

Christina: Please inform your booth contractor to submit their workers' name list and ID copies one week earlier before the booth construction because the Exhibition Center should issue Access Cards for their workers. Workers should enter the Center with Access Cards.

Ivy Xie: I see. How much should we pay for each card?

Christina: RMB50 yuan. We have sent the rules and regulations of booth design and installation to exhibitors. The maximum height of the booth is the key point of the regulations. Please tell your contractor.

Ivy Xie: OK. And I'd like to know if we can get on-site service for additional furniture or other facilities at the exhibition.

Christina: Of course, but they will be subject to a surcharge of 20%.

Ivy Xie: By the way, can you provide accommodation service?

Christina: Yeah. We can accommodate the exhibitors' needs.

Ivy Xie: Oh, I see. Thank you.

Christina: With pleasure.

Unit 3　Module 3

(Background) Steven Li from South West company placed an order with SKY Furniture Trading Company at the Canton Fair last year. Ivy is making a phone call to invite him to attend the coming exhibition at the Canton Fair.

(Scene) At Ivy's office.

Steven Li: Hello, This is South West company. Can I help you?

Ivy Xie: Yes, I'm Ivy from SKY Furniture Trading Company. Can I speak to Steven?

Steven Li: Hello, Ivy. I haven't seen you for a year. How is everything going?

Ivy Xie: Pretty good. I'm calling to invite you to the 128th Canton Fair, to be held in Guangzhou, from October 15 to 31, 2020.

Steven Li: Great. We made orders with your company last year, and the furniture sells well. We received lots of positive comments from the buyers.

Ivy Xie: That's wonderful. Our company has developed some new furniture including kitchen appliances. We hope you will attend our trade show.

Steven Li: Do you have the list of your new products?

Ivy Xie: Yes, I will send our product catalogue and information to your mailbox later.

Steven Li: Thank you. Please send them to SWC@163.com.

Ivy Xie: This exhibition will provide opportunities to everybody interested in SKY furniture, and our new products and demand in the world market will also be shown in the exhibition.

Steven Li: It's so good.

Ivy Xie: Wish you a part of this exhibition. Our booth number is A-F-307, 308.

Steven Li: It's worth going. Thanks for your invitation.

Ivy Xie: Looking forward to seeing you at the exhibition. Thank you.

Unit 4   Module 1

(Background) Ivy Xie as an exhibitor from SKY Furniture Trading Company and George Parker as a visitor from ABC company are participating in the China Import and Export Fair (also known as the Canton Fair). At the exhibition booth, Ivy manages to attract George's interest in some furniture of her company.

(Scene) At the Canton Fair.

Ivy: Good morning. Welcome to our booth. What can I do for you?

George: Good morning. There is a variety of furniture showed at your booth and I like the design and style.

Ivy: Thanks for your interest. Would you like to sit down and know more about our company and products?

George: Er... I am in a hurry.

Ivy: 10 minutes will be OK and you are sure to find it worthwhile.

George: OK.

Ivy: I am Ivy, a salesperson from SKY Furniture Trading Company, and here is my business card.

George: Here is mine. I'm George. Nice to meet you!

Ivy: Please take a seat. What would you like to drink, coffee, black tea or Coca Cola?

George: No, thanks.

Ivy: OK, let's get down to business. May I introduce our company and products to you first?

George: Yes, please.

Ivy: We have been one of the leading manufacturers of office furniture in China since 1998 and we supply file cabinets, office desks and chairs with US$ 18 million worth of products exported last year. MacDonald and Huawei are among our distinguished clients.

George: It sounds great!

Ivy: We have various kinds of styles and sizes for you to choose from and offer custom-made products as well. Here is our catalogue and those on page 1 to 5 are all our best-selling products.

George: They look attractive. May I have a look at the samples?

Ivy: Sure. Come with me. Here they are.

George: This chair looks very modern. Does it have any specific functions?

Ivy: Yes, it slides easily. The wheels are very strong and smooth. The best thing about this chair is that it is with Ergonomic Backrests and a breathable Padded Seat, which makes the sitter keep in the right aligned position and feel very comfortable in the prolonged work. You may have a try now.

George: Wow, it feels great!

Ivy: What's more, it is made of imported materials, very light and easy to carry.

George: Yes, you are right! I am sure my boss will like it. May I keep your catalog?

Ivy: Sure.

George: Oh, I have to leave now. Thanks for your help! I will bring my boss Andy Smith here tomorrow morning for further information.

Ivy: My pleasure. Look forward to seeing you!

George: Bye!

Ivy: Bye!

Unit 4　Module 2

(Background) David Kilmer from East Coast company looking for suppliers of office furniture visited the booth of SKY Furniture Trading Company at the Canton Fair where Ivy Xie received him. As David will be leaving soon, Ivy invited David and his colleague, Daisy for dinner, intending to establish business relations with him.

(Scene) At a restaurant in Guangzhou.

Ivy: Welcome, David and Daisy! I am so glad you come.

David: It's very kind of you to invite us.

Daisy: Many thanks for your invitation.

Ivy: Take your seat, please.

David: To tell the truth, I'm a bit nervous now, as I know nothing of Chinese table manners. It would be a shame to make blunders.

Ivy: Don't worry. As for table manners, there is only one rule you must observe, that's to make yourself at home. I hope the food we've ordered suits your taste.

David: Thank you very much for such a splendid dinner.

Ivy: Please help yourself, everybody.

David: Thank you. It certainly looks very delicious.

Ivy: David, you will be leaving soon. Is your trip to this fair fruitful?

David: Yes, there has been a really wide range of goods on display and most of the prices are reasonable.

Ivy: Have you found anything that particularly interests you?

David: Yes, we are interested in your items AS6 and AS18. The designs are all original. I am sure they'll be quite popular with young customers in our country.

Ivy: Yes, you are right. Items AS6 and AS18 are our latest designs. They are also popular with young consumers here. I am sure they will sell well in your market, too.

David: We hope so.

Ivy: May I know when we can have your order?

David: Honestly, you can have it tomorrow, as I sent your products to my boss and he replied this morning that they are just what we are looking for.

Ivy: I am very glad to hear that. Thank you so much!

(A waiter brings soup.)

Ivy: Here comes the soup. Have a try, please.

David: Wow, it's so delicious! Tell me, Ms. Ivy. How come it tastes so extraordinary while there is nothing in it but just clear water?

Ivy: (Chuckles.) This is the Cantonese style of soup called long-stewed soup, "Lao Huo Liang Tang" in Chinese. We just drink the soup without eating the contents and we have it before the main dishes.

David: Wow, so special! It's the first time that I've had the soup. **(Thumbs up.)**

Ivy: All right. May I propose a toast to our long friendly cooperation?

David: I couldn't agree more. Cheers!

Unit 4　Module 3

(Background) David Kilmer from East Coast company placed an order with SKY Furniture Trading Company at the Canton Fair. David is going to leave Guangzhou and Ivy makes him a phone call to fix a time to see him off.

(Scene) At Ivy's office.

Ivy: Hello, can I speak to David Kilmer?

David: Speaking, please!

Ivy: This is Ivy Xie from SKY Furniture Trading Company.

David: Hi, Ivy, I remember we've just finished an order at the booth at the Canton Fair.

Ivy: Yes, we had a wonderful meeting.

David: It's been a rewarding trip! Thank you for everything, Ivy.

Ivy: It's my pleasure. I am very glad that you enjoy your stay in China.

David: Yes, everything is just perfect.

Ivy: We have a VIP car ready for you. When do you need to leave?

George: For an international flight, it is required to check in two hours in advance, so I need to leave my hotel at 14:00 tomorrow.

Ivy: How much luggage will you bring?

George: I have a carry-on, a purse and a large suitcase.

Ivy: Not too much, so a small but quite comfortable car would be OK for you. May I know where your terminal is?

George: I need to be dropped off on the second level of the International Terminal since I am flying to London by Qatar Airways.

Ivy: Shall I drop you off at the airport?

George: No, thank you. I know you are quite busy these days and have a lot of work to deal with.

Ivy: Thank you for your thoughtfulness! It's a pity that I can't see you off at the airport.

George: It's OK.

Ivy: So,the driver will pick you up at the hotel lobby at 14:00 tomorrow, right?

George: Yes. Thank you!

Ivy: My pleasure. Have a nice trip!

Unit 5   Module 1

(Background) Sales manager Baron Li from SKY Furniture Trading Company is introducing his company to George Parker from ABC company.

(Scene) At the Canton Fair.

Baron: Hello, Mr. Parker. Welcome to our company. I'm Baron Li, sales manager of SKY Furniture Trading Company.

George: Nice to meet you, Mr. Li.

Baron: Nice to meet you, too. You can call me Baron.

George: Thank you, Baron. And you can call me George.

Baron: Thank you, George.

George: My Boss Andy Smith has something urgent to deal with and he asked me to know more about your company and products.

Baron: Thank you for your interest. Now allow me to introduce our company to you.

George: Great. I have already had a general idea about your company through the Internet, and it will be better for me to know more about it through your introduction.

Baron: Sure. As you know, our company is a furniture trading company, which is located in Foshan, Guangdong province.

George: Yes, Foshan is a beautiful place and I have heard that Foshan is regarded as a "Chinese furniture manufacturing base".

Baron: Yes, you are right. There is a staff of about 300 in our company. We aim at setting design, development, production, and sales service as a whole, supplying modern fashionable comfortable furniture.

George: That's why I'm interested in your company.

Baron: Our company's unique people-oriented culture attracts and retains outstanding talents, providing quality service and driving product innovation for customers. Later you will know you won't miss the bold and beautiful product catalogues in showrooms.

George: That sounds good. I am looking forward to the showroom.

Baron: Our products are endowed with the practical value and aesthetic value which the social mainstream family-oriented furniture calls for.

George: Yes, I can feel that.

Baron: Our designers have always been pursuing a good combination of art and fashion, nature and environmental protection, simplicity and amenity.

George: It is very good when you are taking the environment-friendly concept into your production.

Baron: And you can see that the Chinese modern furniture production technology is used to make our furniture series. Fine craftsmanship and beautiful designs have built up an enviable reputation, and high quality makes us a manufacturing leader in the Foshan district.

George: Oh, that's perfect.

Baron: And we pay special attention to absorbing foreign fashion furniture design concepts.

George: Yes, it's much better if your company is planning to expand your overseas market.

Baron: Also, we can leverage our buying power to maintain the demands of our loyal customers.

George: I'm hoping to visit your showroom.

Unit 5 Module 2

(Background) In the showroom, sales manager Baron Li from SKY Furniture Trading Company

is introducing the major products to George Parker from ABC company.

(Scene) In the showroom.

Baron: George, welcome to our showroom.

George: Thank you, I'm glad to be here.

Baron: This way, please. Our products are categorized into two types: cloth products and leather ones, including sofas, chairs and beds.

George: Good.

Baron: You can find we combine the elements of stainless steel, steel and aluminum with cloth and leather in a very comfortable way. Over there, you can see the uniqueness of this technology from sofa series, chair series, bed series and leisure furniture series. We have cemented ourselves in the hearts of our customers by offering products that meet style expectations, price ranges and excellent quality to achieve the home culture—A home of your dream with beauty and comfort.

George: Wow, great!

Baron: For the sofa series, there are 2-seat sofas, 3-seat sofas and loveseats(小双人沙发).

George: In our market, the 3-seat sofa is very popular among the middle-aged couples to use at their homes while the young couples prefer the loveseats.

Baron: Yes, when we design these types, we have considered that.

Baron: For the sofa series, the theme of the major products this year is "the light of the city". George, you can see the sectional sofa(组合沙发)in front of us. It is named "Sydney". For the sectional sofa, we have corner(转角), right arm chaise(右扶手躺椅), 4-piece(4件套), U-shaped(U形) and L-shaped(L形).

George: How about that sofa, what do you call it?

Baron: We call this set right arm chaise 4-Piece U-shaped sectional sofa (右边有扶手躺椅、整体形态呈U形的组合沙发).

George: Yes, I like this sectional sofa. Look, the color is white and gray, combining cloth and leather with the metal element of stainless steel, steel and aluminum in an excellent way.

Baron: Yes, this sectional sofa is very popular. We have already received many orders from clients from North America, Middle East, South Africa, etc. I am sure you will sell it well in your country too.

George: In that case, I'm thinking of placing a trial order. Oh, what is that over there?

Baron: It's an ottoman. There are two types, one is storage ottoman(储物凳)and the other one is bench. Usually, in many houses, an ottoman can be used as a coffee table(茶几). It is a fashion to put it in in the living room. The bench can be settled in the bedroom.

George: When I place an order, I would like to order the storage ottoman too，because I am sure it will become popular in our market.

Baron: Yes, it's a good choice to do that.

George: Thank you. Great minds think alike.

Baron: Here come the chair series: chair sets, dining chairs, ladderback chairs and folding chairs. Meanwhile, we also offer slipcovers and cushions.

George: I am interested in folding chairs. Maybe I will put them on my ordering list.

Baron: Here come the bed series. Usually, we have bed frames(床架)and headboards(床头板).

There are four sizes: twin(单人床), full(标准双人床), queen(大双人床)and king(加大双人床).

George: Yes, these beds are good.

Baron: That's all for the products displayed in this showroom. Actually, we have one more showroom in the other part of the city. If you are willing to go there, we can fix a time.

George: I would like to. How about next Monday?

Baron: No problem!

George: Oh, I have to go. Thank you for your time!

Baron: It's my pleasure! Remember me to Andy Smith! See you next Monday!

George: Sure. See you!

Unit 5   Module 3

(Background) Baron Li, the Sales Manager from SKY Company, is introducing the exhibits to George Parker, a visitor from ABC Company.

(Scene) At the showroom in SKY Company.

Baron: Mr. Parker, how do you think of this series?

George: I appreciate the concept of the series "City Lights" very much. It reminds me of the time when I studied in Sydney ten years ago. But the couch is not what I'm looking for this time.

Baron: Then may I ask what kind of furniture would you like to see?

George: I'm mainly looking for office chairs and tables. As for other items, well, I'd also like to have a look if they're suitable.

Baron: OK. As for the office chairs, our company has developed two new designs this year. We can have a look over there.

George: OK.

Baron: This office chair is called Yoho, whose design originates from the concept of "harmony" of traditional Chinese culture. It takes its name from the Chinese meaning for leisurely life.

George: That's great. I'm a fan of Chinese culture.

Baron: It is designed to follow the human body's flexibility and every postural movement being perfectly ergonomic and highly functional. The headrest and armrest adaptability are complemented to the aerodynamic structure and its padded support in the lumbar zone fulfills a good posture and greater comfort.

George: Cool! May I sit down and have a try?

Baron: Sure.

George: It's good.

Baron: If you are tired from busy work, you can also adjust the back of the chair slightly, so that the chair, from the headrest to the backrest to the armrest, can support you in all directions. Just like this. How do you feel, Mr. Parker?

George: Wow! It's comfortable.

Baron: Do you feel like a child in the mother's arms?

George: Yeah, right! Exactly!

Baron: This office chair is equipped with a multi-functional chassis imported from Taiwan, which can adjust the seat depth and the tilt angle of the headrest and backrest, to achieve comfortable and healthy use for users of various body sizes.

George: Awesome! That explains why it is so comfortable.

Baron: The chair uses internationally popular color elements and environmentally friendly fabrics, and is molded by one-step injection.

George: Excellent. Just now you said your company has developed two new chair designs.

Baron: Yes, here is another new design that looks like a flamingo from the side view.

George: Very interesting and graceful.

Baron: It has the same equipment and material as the former one, and both of these two designs come in four colors: black, gray, blue and red.

George: Good. How much are they?

Baron: Could you tell me how many you will order? The minimum order quantity is 100 pieces, and the price changes according to your order.

George: I can't make the decision right now. I have to report to my boss before I order.

Baron: I see, Mr. Parker. Here is my name card. Please contact me any time if you make the decision, so that I can send you the quotation as soon as possible.

George: Sure. Here is mine. Nice talking with you, Mr. Li. See you.

Baron: Bye.

Unit 6　Module 1

(Background) At the Canton Fair, Andy from ABC company is interested in some furniture from Baron's company, SKY Furniture Trading Company, which he visited yesterday. So today he goes back to the exhibition booth of SKY Furniture Trading Company and intends to work on the price with Baron.

(Scene) At the Canton Fair.

Andy: Hi, Baron.

Baron: Hello Andy. Nice to see you again. Is there anything I can do for you?

Andy: Yes. After checking your catalogue, we are interested in your coffee table CT25008. What's the price of it?

Baron: Thank you for your inquiry. I'm glad to quote you for the coffee table CT25008. It's US$20 FOB Shenzhen, US$24 CIF Liverpool per piece.

Andy: You can't be serious. That's too expensive.

Baron: Our price is reasonable. As you can see, our products are of high quality and in a delicate design.

Andy: But the price still seems a little bit higher than we expected.

Baron: Frankly speaking, we've already given you our rock-bottom price because we are sincere in our cooperation. But we always try to be flexible. We might be able to trim a little off that.

Andy: Good.

Baron: We'll give you a 10% discount. That's the best price we can offer. Please note that our quotation is much lower than the current market price.

Andy: That's an attractive offer, but we hope that the price can be reduced by 15%.

Baron: Wow, you are driving a hard bargain. What we've offered is a fair price. You know, we have got certain fixed costs to cover. Besides, the cost of materials is rising a lot recently.

Andy: I know and that's why we only ask for a 15% discount. The problem is , at your price, we can hardly make any profit and it will be difficult to open our market in our country. Due to the pandemic of Covid-19, the coffee tables' sales volume in our country is dropping sharply.

Baron: All right. Let's split the difference and call it 12% off to conclude the business. Is that Ok?

Andy: Sounds good to me!

Baron: Great! I am glad we finally agree upon the price. But I have to report to the head office for the final decision. We'll reply to you tomorrow.

Andy: Sure, looking forward to your reply. Bye.

Baron: Bye.

Unit 6   Module 2

(Background) At the Canton Fair, Andy, from ABC company, and Baron, from SKY Furniture Trading Company, finally reach an agreement on the price. They move on to have a further discussion on payment terms.

(Scene) At the booth at the Canton Fair.

Andy: Well, I'm glad we are likely to conclude the first transaction with you soon. Since the problems of price and quantity have been settled, now let's talk about the terms of payment.

Baron: OK.

Andy: What mode of payment do you prefer?

Baron: The only mode of payment we can accept is payment via a confirmed and irrevocable L/C payable against the presentation of shipment documents.

Andy: I'm sorry that you insist on payment by L/C. Could you possibly make an exception and accept D/A or D/P?

Baron: I'm afraid not. We don't want to run the risk of losing money.

Andy: Well, frankly speaking, a letter of credit would increase the cost of my imports. When we open a letter of credit with a bank, we'll have to pay a margin. That will not only tie up our money but also increase our costs .

Baron: I'm sorry. For future dealings we may allow other ways of payment such as D/P, but not now. In your case, I think you can consult your bank and see if they agree to reduce the required margin to a minimum.

Andy: I know, but still there will be bank charges and fix expenses in opening an L/C. If you could accept D/A or D/P, it would help me greatly.

Baron: Well, I'm afraid I'll disappoint you. As you know, an irrevocable L/C provides us additional protection of the bank's guarantee. That's why payment by L/C is required for our exports. This is also the usual practice adopted internationally.

Andy: I see your point. Let's meet each other halfway. What do you think if we make half the payment by L/C and the balance by D/P?

Baron: Well, Ms. Andy, I regret to tell you that it's not workable for us. Sorry about that! As I've said before, the only method of payment we accept is L/C. L/C at sight is what we request from all our customers for such commodities, especially with our new customers. If we make an exception here, we cannot know where to stop.

Andy: All right. It looks like I have no other choice but to accept 100% L/C payment.

Baron: I'm afraid so. For a new client, we can't accept any terms of payment other than L/C.

Andy: OK. Do you have any other special requirements for the L/C?

Baron: Oh yes. We require documentary credit to be opened at the Bank of China.

Andy: Right.

Baron: And one more thing, the L/C should reach us 30 days before the date of delivery. Therefore, you should open the L/C as soon as possible. Otherwise, the shipment will be delayed.

Andy: OK, that's understood.

Baron: Great! Thank you very much for your cooperation.

Unit 6　Module 3

(Background) Having settled the terms of payment, now Andy from ABC company, and Baron from SKY Furniture Trading Company, get to talk over shipment, packing and insurance, etc.

(Scene) At the Canton Fair.

Andy: Now Baron, let's come to the delivery. Can you make a prompt shipment? We want to get our goods ready for the Christmas sales season.

Baron: Well, I'm afraid it's difficult for us to do that. As you know, those products are our best sellers this year. So in fact, we don't have the amount of the products in stock right now. But I promise you that these days we'll have workers working in three shifts so as to step up the production against your orders.

Andy: Then when is the earliest we can effect the shipment? You see, we have to catch the sales season.

Baron: I see your point. Our shipping department told me yesterday that the liner space for Europe had been fully booked up to the end of this month. So I'm afraid we'll have to wait until early next month, that is, early November.

Andy: That would be too late. Is there any chance of transshipment to be allowed? Or do you have any other suggestions?

Baron: Well, I don't think transshipment is a good option because it adds to the expenses, risks of damage and sometimes may even delay arrival. We are operating a container service from Guangzhou, Shanghai to European sea routes. But I have to tell you that it's a little bit costly.

Andy: If transshipment is not a good option, it seems that the container is the last resort.

Baron: If the container vessel is your final choice, I'd like to tell you that there will be one heading for Europe at the end of this month. Besides, it's not fully booked up and the remaining vessel space is enough for your lot. What's more, we'll have sufficient time to get the goods ready for container shipment by that time.

Andy: That's great! It's the best solution for both of us. How are you going to pack our goods?

Baron: The goods are packed in cartons. Coffee tables are packed 2 pieces into a carton. Besides, foam plastics are used to protect the goods against the press.

Andy: Could you strengthen the cartons with double straps? We all know strong packing will protect the goods against any possible damage during transit.

Baron: No problem! We'll make sure that all items are carefully packed so that they can reach you in good condition.

Andy: Good! And how about insurance?

Baron: Well, as usual, the goods have been insured in W.A. terms. Premium will be added to the invoice amount together with freight charges.

Andy: That's understood. Thank you very much!

Baron: My pleasure!

Unit 6   Module 4

(Background) After a large of problems regarding the purchase of bundling terms has been settled, Andy from ABC company is on the discussion with Baron from SKY Furniture Trading Company on concrete contract terms for the import business of furniture from China.

(Scene) At the Canton Fair.

Baron: After all the discussions, we finally reach a basic agreement on the problems that should be worked out.

Andy: That's true. I'm so happy with the progress we've made.

Baron: Me too. Shall we sign the contract now?

Andy: Yes, but we'd better have another check to avoid arguing over some minor problems in the days to come.

Baron: That's a good idea. OK, let's get down to business. Let's check all the items and make sure that no important items are overlooked.

Andy: Right.

Baron: First of all, as for the format, the contract has been written in both Chinese and English. Both languages are equally effective.

Andy: Yes.

Baron: There are two of the originals of the contract. Here's a copy for you to check.

Andy: Thank you! Please excuse me and I need a moment to go over it first.

Baron: Definitely. Take your time.

Andy: Thank you.

(after 15 minutes)

Andy: All right. Hmm, you've done a great job. Almost all the clauses are clearly stated as we've discussed earlier.

Baron: Thank you! Do you have any problem with it?

Andy: Yes, I'm afraid that there are still some clauses that might need further discussion.

Baron: Well, in that case, we can spend some time on them and see what we can do with them for our mutual benefit.

Andy: Yes. Firstly, let's read Clause Two about packing. I want to double-check that our products will be shipped in containers, right?

Baron: Yes.

Andy: Great.

Baron: As for shipment, if we can't get all our products ready before the end of this month, would you allow us to make partial shipments?

Andy: No problem. But I still hope that you can make every effort to step up the production, as we've discussed earlier.

Baron: Sure. I really appreciate your understanding! Do you have any other questions?

Andy: No. I think everything is in order here.

Baron: Well then, all that's left is to sign our names.

Andy: Yes, I'm so pleased that we close the deal finally.

Baron: Me too. To be honest, I've been looking forward to this moment for a long time.

Andy: I hope the contract will lead to years of pleasant cooperation.

Baron: That would be great! Let's propose a toast to our cooperation!

Andy: Cheers!

Unit 7　Module 1

(Background) Ivy Xie is an exhibitor from SKY Furniture Trading Company and Baron Li is the sales manager from the same company. At the exhibition booth, Baron and Ivy are talking about the dismantlement.

(Scene) At the Canton Fair.

Baron: Good morning, Ivy.

Ivy: Morning, Baron.

Baron: The exhibit will end in three days. Have you arranged the move-out?

Ivy: Yes, I have hired an experienced team to help us with the dismantling.

Baron: Great! According to the regulations and rules on dismantlement, here are some instructions we need to follow.

Ivy: All right, I will take them down.

Baron: First of all, we are not allowed to dismantle, amend, destroy or deface the exiting building or all permanent facilities.

Ivy: Are the electrical appliances included?

Baron: I am afraid so. In addition, the floor and walls as well as the wall panels of the booth may not be nailed or holed.

Ivy: Ok, I will keep an eye on it. What else?

Baron: For moving our furniture outside the exhibition halls, pushcarts with rubber or nylon wheels are requested.

Ivy: I will see to it and keep you posted.

Baron: Thanks. And we must get the release form in advance.

Ivy: Oh, I almost forget the release form! I'll go and get it this afternoon.

Baron: Do remember that workers only with a valid Pass for booth dismantlement may enter the exhibition halls and must go through the security check.

Ivy: Got it! I will make sure the team will be informed, so we won't end up paying a penalty charge.

Baron: You are a great help. Do you have any questions?

Ivy: Yes, I am concerned about the accessories taken down. What are we going to do with them?

Baron: Well, for those which can be reused somewhere else, transport them back to the warehouse; for the rest of them, move them to the landfills.

Ivy: All right. It seems we need to use more recyclable materials next time.

Baron: That's a good idea.

Ivy: By the way, what's the deadline for dismantling? And what can we do if we need extra time for dismantling?

Baron: If we need more time, we can apply for it at the Customer Service Counter, but we have to pay extra money for the delay and the charge is RMB 1000 per stand per day.

Ivy: It is a bit expensive for the delay. We'd better finish everything before the deadline.

Baron: Exactly!

Unit 7　Module 2

(Background) Jeffery Smith, a staffer from the Fair Committee, is responsible for collecting feedback on the Fair from the exhibitors. He is asking the opinions of Ivy Xie.

(Scene) At the booth at the Canton Fair.

Jeffery: Hello, Ivy. Nice to see you again.

Ivy: Hi, Jeffery. Nice to see you too.

Jeffery: I wonder if you could spare me a few minutes.

Ivy: Sure. What can I do for you?

Jeffery: Thanks. You see, I have collected the feedback questionnaires from the exhibitors, and I know there are things we need to improve. Since it is the fifth time you have attended the fair, I'd like to get more feedback from you. So what do you think of the exhibition?

Ivy: It is very successful. Our participation proved to be worthwhile and productive and we have attained many new contacts.

Jeffery: I am glad to hear that. What about the organization and planning of the fair?

Ivy: No complaints. We are satisfied with the arrangements.

Jeffery: That is encouraging. Could you give us some suggestions so that we could do a better job next time?

Ivy: Well, I think it would be better to have more foreign media. We always wanted to make more international exposure of our corporate image to attract more foreign customers.

Jeffery: Thank you for your suggestion. The fair has been promoted in various channels this year and has attracted more visitors from abroad. With the promotion, I believe we will attract more foreign media next year.

Ivy: It's good to hear that.

Jeffery: Is there any other thing we can improve?

Ivy: Another thing is that with the number of the audience increasing, sometimes the exhibition halls were overcrowded. Some visitors just sat on our chairs which were our exhibits.

Jeffery: I am sorry. The number of audiences was beyond our expectations. We will reserve a larger space next year and try to improve our service.

Ivy: Then I think I want to come again next year.

Jeffery: I am looking forward to seeing you next fair.

Unit 7   Module 3

(Background) Baron Li, the sales manager of SKY Furniture Trading Company, has just returned from the Canton Fair. He is reporting the results to the vice president of the company, Nicholas Court.

(Scene) At Nicholas' office.

Baron: (Knock at the door) May I come in?

Nicholas: Yes. Please come in and have a seat.

Baron: Mr. court, would you please spare me a few minutes? I'd like to report the results of the trade fair to you.

Nicholas: Sure. So how did it go?

Baron: The fair was a huge success and absolutely beyond our expectations. We've established many new contacts.

Nicholas: Great! What were the total sales and the profit rate?

Baron: The total sales amounted to 5 million dollars, which is 600 thousand dollars more than that of last year. And the profit rate reached 15 percent.

Nicholas: Your team did an excellent job. What about the visitors? What did they think of our new products?

Baron: The number of visitors has increased dramatically this year. Most of them, especially the international participants were interested in the chairs made of environment-friendly material. And that is why we signed more contracts this year.

Nicholas: It seems that we did have very good brand exposure and we have reached our objectives in attending the fair including making connections and expanding sales.

Baron: We did receive positive responses from the visitors.

Nicholas: That's impressive. Are there any improvements we can make for the exhibition in the future?

Baron: Yes. One thing is that we need to prepare more catalogues printed in both Chinese and English.

Nicholas: I think it is quite necessary as visitors are increasing year by year. What else?

Baron: Well, is it possible to add more budget for the fair?

Nicholas: You mean you need more budget for the next exhibition?

Baron: I am afraid so.

Nicholas: Well, can you produce a written report on the results of the fair by next Friday? Then we may talk about the budget according to the results at the sum-up meeting?

Baron: No problem. I will get down to it.

Nicholas: By the way, don't forget to follow up the uncontracted potential customers as well as the contracted customers.

Baron: Sure.

Nicholas: Thank you for your hard work. Well done, Baron.

Baron: With pleasure. We'll try to keep up the good work.

Unit 8   Module 1

(Background) Two days have passed since the Canton Fair ended. Ivy Xie, an exhibitor from SKY Furniture Trading Company, and the receptionist Serena Wang are asked to come to Baron Li's office to take up new tasks.

(Scene) At Baron's office.

(Knocks at the door)

Baron: Come in, please.

Ivy & Serena: Good afternoon, Baron.

Baron: Good afternoon, ladies. How is everything going these two days after the Canton Fair?

Ivy: Pretty good. Visitors and inquirers are much more than ever before.

Serena: And two European buyers intend to place orders this afternoon.

Baron: That's good news. Ivy, please arrange your department staff for the after-show marketing activities as soon as possible.

Ivy: OK. I've finished all the thank-you emails to the visitors who left name cards during the Canton Fair.

Serena: But is it too soon for the after-show marketing activities, for the Canton Fair has just been over for only 2 days?

Baron: Nope. It's just the right time to begin. Serena, you have joined our company for only several months and it is the first time for you to attend the Canton Fair. You could ask Ivy for more advice about marketing activities. She learns fast and is very good at it now.

Ivy: I agree with Baron. As it goes, make hay while the sun shines. It would be too late to follow up if we don't take actions soon.

Serena: I see. We're likely to lose our leads to other competitors if we don't take the initiative.

Baron: That's right. Ivy, have a meeting with all the marketing members tomorrow morning and make clear the key points of the marketing activities after the exhibition.

Ivy: OK.

(Ivy and Serena go out of Baron's office and back to their team office.)

Serena: It seems that the after-show follow-up requires lots of skills.

Ivy: Yeah, how much we can benefit from an exhibition, to a great extent, depends on how well the follow-up can be done.

Serena: Then how do you usually follow up?

Ivy: For foreign buyers, emails and phone calls have been the most commonly used ways for the last two decades. Recently, we also communicate more on social networks.

Serena: What can we say or write for the first step of follow-up? We can't urge them to place an order, right?

Ivy: Definitely not. What to say or write depends on which level we grade the buyers at.

Serena: Level? Do we grade the buyers? But how?

Ivy: Yes. Generally, we grade them according to their urgency of order placement and purchasing power.

Serena: That is to say, the higher the buyer's level is, the more quickly we should follow up.

Ivy: That's it. Only more timely follow-up and more attention will make the clients feel more valued. In that way, they are more likely to be won over.

Serena: Just now you told Baron that you've finished all the thank-you emails to the visitors who left name cards on the first day. So do we usually express our gratitude first?

Ivy: Yes, we do. We thank them for coming to our booth the first time, and then follow up a second time one week later according to the situation of the booth reception.

Serena: How long does it usually take to follow up?

Ivy: The higher a buyer's level is, the faster the follow-up should be. While for the buyer at a lower level, the period will be relatively longer. Thus more patience is necessary for after-show marketing activities.

Serena: The after-show marketing activities are completely not as simple as I thought. Let me assist you with the follow-up business from this moment on.

Ivy: OK. Although skills and patience are indispensable, the more you do, the more experience you'll get.

Serena: I hope one day I can do as well as you do.

Ivy: You will.

Unit 8　Module 2

(Background) George Parker from ABC Company was so satisfied with the products of SKY Furniture Trading Company at the Canton Fair that he placed an order at the fair. But later in the process of manufacturing, there was something wrong with the raw material supply. Ivy from the SKY Company is calling George Parker to negotiate about this problem.

(Scene) At Ivy's office.

George: Hello, George speaking.

Ivy: Good morning, Mr. Parker. This is Ivy from SKY Company.

George: Hi, Ivy. So glad to receive your phone call. How are you?

Ivy: I'm good. Thank you, and you?

George: Everything goes well. So are you calling to inform me that you are ready for the shipment?

Ivy: Well, Mr. Smith, I'm afraid not. Here is what's happening now. Compared with the Canton Fair in the previous years, the order is much larger this year. Our raw material supplier can't supply continuously, which may lead to the shipment delay of the products.

George: Oh, that's too bad. You know, many dealers have already placed an order with my company. If I can't get the goods on time, I won't be able to deliver them to my clients. Have you got any solution?

Ivy: Firstly, I'm so sorry for bringing trouble to you. After discussing with my boss, we now have two solutions for you to choose from. Let's see which one you prefer.

George: OK.

Ivy: One is that we offer you a 5% discount for the whole order due to the shipment delay.

George: But I'm still worried that some of my dealers may cancel their orders for not being able to get the goods on time. And the other one?

Ivy: Then the other one is partial shipment. For the completed goods, we can arrange to deliver them these days. It's nearly one month ahead of the time in the contract. As for the rest, we can only deliver behind time. But we promise to give priority to your production as soon as we get the raw materials.

George: It's good that part of my order can arrive ahead of time. How late will the rest be?

Ivy: Two to three months approximately.

George: Oh, that's a little bit too long. In that case, I'm not sure how many of my dealers can wait until the second arrival of goods.

Ivy: I'm sorry it is truly awkward. But we believe that the skillful manufacture and user-friendly design of our products can make it worth waiting.

George: Only by giving up more profit, can I probably keep these dealers. Give us a 10% discount on the rest part. Is that OK?

Ivy: Mr. Smith, the biggest discount we can offer is 5%, for the cost for the second shipment is borne by our company.

George: But the waiting period of two to three months is too long. If those dealers cancel the orders with me, I may cancel the order of the rest of the goods as well.

Ivy: Well, Mr. Smith, let's say 7% off. That's the lowest price we can go to.

George: Well, that's acceptable, but please try not to delay longer than two months.

Ivy: Sure. We'll prioritize your production.

George: Good. Then let's keep in touch.

Ivy: I'm sorry again for the delay. We'll arrange the shipment for you the moment the production is completed.

George: OK.

Unit 8   Module 3

(Background) Frank Smith, a visitor from JKC Company, showed a great interest in the products of SKY Furniture Trading Company at the Canton Fair. Ivy Xie, a sales girl from SKY Company, once talked with Frank Smith, and now she is trying to follow up on the phone.

(Scene) At Ivy's office.

Ivy: Hello, This is Ivy from SKY Furniture Trading Company. Can I speak to Mr. Smith?

Frank: Speaking, please.

Ivy: Good morning, Mr. Smith. It was so nice to meet you at the Canton Fair last week, and we had a very pleasant conversation.

Frank: Hello, Ivy. The products of your company are very impressive. I was glad to know SKY and the fine furniture at the Canton Fair.

Ivy: Thank you for your recognition of our company and products. Our company has a history of nearly 40 years in developing and manufacturing office furniture, and many products enjoy very good reputation in European and American countries.

Frank: I've got the materials of your company introduction and product catalogue at the fair. I'll read them carefully.

Ivy: Thank you very much. At the fair, you mentioned that you were looking for office chairs. Would you mind if I ask you which design you are interested in?

Frank: Oh, I kind of like the flamingo-shaped chair and the council board.

Ivy: You have a good taste, Mr. Smith. That office chair is a newly-developed design this year, and the council board is a classic style of our company with a very good market in Europe and America.

Frank: Really? The chair is unique in design, and it's quite comfortable to sit in.

Ivy: Yes, this chair is designed conforming to the kinesiology principle. There is a brochure specifically introducing this chair and its series in detail. I'll forward it to you later after this phone call.

Frank: That's great! And please forward me the one introducing the council board as well if there is.

Ivy: Sure! I'll forward both to you. Can I email you through the email box address on your name card?

Frank: Yes.

Ivy: Ok. I'll email you right away. Please give me your feedback if you have any ideas.

Frank: No problem.

国内外主要会展网站、国内外大型会展、国际会展专业术语可扫描下方二维码阅读。

参 考 文 献

[1] 蔡龙文，黄冬梅. 会展实务英语 [M]. 2版. 北京：对外经济贸易大学出版社，2016.

[2] 李红英. 会展英语实用教程 [M]. 大连：大连理工大学出版社，2008.

[3] 李世平，陈颖. 会展英语 [M]. 2版. 北京：北京大学出版社，2020.

[4] 龚东庆. 会展布局与设计 [M]. 北京：高等教育出版社，2007.

[5] 郭英之. 会展概论 [M]. 北京：旅游教育出版社，2007.

[6] 黄晓彤，等. 会展英语 [M]. 北京：外语教学与研究出版社，2012.

[7] Lan Wood，Paul Sanderson，Anne Williams, 等. 新编剑桥商务英语 [M]. 北京：经济科学出版社，2005.

[8] 雷兵，杨晓梅. 会展英语 [M]. 大连：东北财经大学出版社，2009.

[9] 蓝星，冯修文. 会展实务英语·口语 [M]. 上海：上海交通大学出版社，2011.

[10] 瞿杰. 会展实务英语 [M]. 天津：南开大学出版社，2011.

[11] 任红霞. 商务会展英语口语快速突破 [M]. 北京：中国水利水电出版社，2019.

[12] 沈银针. 会展英语 [M]. 北京：中国人民大学出版社，2010.

[13] 宋炜，董云鹏. 国际会展实务：双语教程 [M]. 广州：广东高等教育出版社，2017.

[14] 王芳. 会展英语 [M]. 3版. 大连：东北财经大学出版社，2020.

[15] 吴建华，肖璇. 会展英语口语教程 [M]. 广州：世界图书出版广东有限公司，2012.

[16] 杨翠萍. 会展英语 [M]. 上海：上海交通大学出版社，2010.

[17] 张玛丽. 国际会展英语 [M]. 北京：中国纺织出版社，2018.

[18] 朱学宁，杨国民，舒立志. 会展实务英语教程 [M]. 北京：北京师范大学出版社，2011.